THE BACKGROUND OF MODERN POETRY

E·P·DUTTON & CO. INC.
1852 1952
CELEBRATING 100 YEARS OF PUBLISHING

THE BACKGROUND
OF
MODERN POETRY

by

J. ISAACS

NEW YORK

E. P. DUTTON & CO., INC.

1952

Copyright, 1952, by E. P. Dutton & Co., Inc.
All Rights Reserved. Printed in the U.S.A.

FIRST EDITION

No part of this book may be reproduced
in any form without permission in writing
from the publisher except by a reviewer
who wishes to quote brief passages in connection with a review written for inclusion
in magazine or newspaper or radio broadcast.

PN
1271
I 75

Library of Congress Catalog Card No. 52-5313

32384

TO
THE MEMORY OF
ISAAC ROSENBERG
AND
ALAN PORTER

Contents

ACKNOWLEDGMENTS

Acknowledgment and thanks are tendered to the following for their courtesy in permitting quotation of copyright matter:

Aldington, Richard: *Evening*. Reprinted from THE POEMS OF RICHARD ALDINGTON, Doubleday & Co., Inc. Copyright by Richard Aldington, 1928.

Crane, Hart: *At Melville's Tomb*. Reprinted by permission of Liveright Publishing Corporation from THE COLLECTED POEMS OF HART CRANE. Copyright by Liveright, Inc., 1933.

Eliot, T. S.: lines from *The Love Song of J. Alfred Prufrock;* from *The Waste Land,* from *Sweeney among the Nightingales, Mr. Eliot's Sunday Service,* and *Whispers of Immortality*. Reprinted from COLLECTED POEMS 1909–1935, Harcourt, Brace & Co. Copyright by T. S. Eliot, 1936.

Eliot, T. S.: lines from *Little Gidding*. Reprinted from FOUR QUARTETS by permission of Harcourt, Brace & Co. Copyright by T. S. Eliot, 1943.

Frost, Robert: *Dust of Snow*. Reprinted by permission of Henry Holt and Company, Inc. from NEW HAMPSHIRE by Robert Frost. Copyright by Henry Holt and Company, Inc., 1923. Copyright by Robert Frost, 1951.

Lewis, Alun: *The Poet*. Reprinted by permission of The Macmillan Company from RAIDER'S DAWN AND OTHER POEMS by Alun Lewis. Copyright by The Macmillan Company, 1942.

MacNeice, Louis: *Homage to Clichés*. Reprinted by

ACKNOWLEDGMENTS

permission of Random House, Inc., from POEMS 1925–1940 MacNEICE. Copyright by Random House, Inc., 1940.

Pound, Ezra: *Fan-piece for her Imperial Lord* and *In a Station of the Metro*. Reprinted from LUSTRA OF EZRA POUND WITH EARLIER POEMS, Alfred A. Knopf, Inc. Copyright by Ezra Pound, 1917.

Sitwell, Edith: *Still falls the Rain*. Reprinted by permission of Vanguard Press, Inc., from THE CANTICLE OF THE ROSE. Copyright by Edith Sitwell, 1949.

Stevens, Wallace: *Of Modern Poetry*. Reprinted by permission of Alfred A. Knopf, Inc. from PARTS OF A WORLD. Copyright by Wallace Stevens, 1942.

Yeats, W. B.: *The Scholar*. Reprinted by permission of The Macmillan Company from COLLECTED POEMS. Copyright by The Macmillan Company, 1950.

Also to Messrs. William Heinemann, Ltd. for passages from Arthur Symons' THE SYMBOLIST MOVEMENT IN LITERATURE; to Routledge and Kegan Paul, Ltd. for two poems from SPECULATIONS by T. E. Hulme; to Mr. F. S. Flint for *Eau-Forte;* to Mr. John Rodker for *Immanence;* to Mr. T. S. Eliot and Messrs. Faber & Faber, Ltd. for Mr. Eliot's early poems and later criticism; to Mr. L. Aaronson for *Odds and Ends* from CHRIST IN THE SYNAGOGUE.

THE BACKGROUND OF MODERN POETRY

I

How it Strikes a Contemporary

IT is a common complaint that modern poets know nothing of English poetry beyond what Mr. Eliot has taught them or Mr. Leavis has tried to teach them, that they approach their problems without knowing which poetical problems have been tackled before, or indeed that any poetical problems have ever been tackled. They know John Donne because Mr. Eliot asserted his relevance. They know Skelton because Mr. Robert Graves used him, and they know Langland because Gerard Manley Hopkins and Mr. W. H. Auden were aware of him. Certainly some lines of some poets exist afresh, or even for the first time, because Mr. Eliot has quoted them or twisted them or assimilated them. Some leap to the mind immediately:

> But at my back from time to time I hear
> The sound of horns and motors, which shall bring
> Sweeney to Mrs. Porter in the spring.

Or:

> The Chair she sat in, like a burnished throne,
> Glowed on the marble.

Or again:

> Good night, ladies, good night, sweet ladies, good
> night, good night.

This selective awareness of literary relations sets the poet somewhat apart from his public, because there is no common body of reference, and no 'community of belief' on what is meant or demanded by poetry. It is this double community which constitutes a classical age, and its absence makes complete nonsense of the claim that modern poetry has entered a new classical phase, that the battle with romanticism has resulted in a victory for a neo-neo-classicism, a new Age of Reason. 'The heart has its reasons which reason knows nothing of.'

Fortunately, poetical history has a habit of repeating itself. Not only has this crime of modern poetry happened before, but we may go so far as to say that it has always happened. Poetry has always been modern, and its problems actual. English poetry has always been contemporary poetry, and only by looking at it that way can we feel its life.

Literary history as we find it in the textbooks is ludicrously wrong, because it is over-simplified and diagrammatic, and it never answers any of the important questions. The more I burrow into the real history of literature, the more amazed I am at the arrogant statements of literary historians. Their attitude is changing, but it hasn't yet got into the textbooks.

What do we mean by the *real* history of literature? First of all, by literature one means, of course, poetry, and its real history can only be established by separating 'poetry' from the poets. Most histories of poetry are just a chronological sequence of accounts of individual poets. What we need is perspective rather than chronology, based on what was really happening in poetry itself, rather than in certain prominent and successful poets—a history of the turf rather than of winners only, of consumers rather than producers. We need a history of the struggle rather than the achievements, of the process of English poetry as seen by the reading public, and by poets struggling for the glory and dignity of their craft. Literary history is ruthless towards the unsuccessful. I think the poetry of our time will have an advantage in the textbooks of the future, because we are so much more aware of what has been going on, and we have preserved the records of our bewilderment and our debates where previous ages have let them vanish.

One advantage of treating English poetry as perennially contemporary and perennially alive to its problems of craft as distinct from message, craft in the highest and widest sense, is that we can adopt a different time-perspective, indeed we are forced to do so. We must recognise, for instance, that Milton comes, not before Dryden, where he belongs chronologically, but between Dryden and Pope, where he belongs as a poetical force. Milton was never a contemporary *poet*, in our sense of contemporary, but his *poetry* became a force in a new contemporary setting. We must see, too, that Chaucer comes, not as a primitive figure of the Italian Renaissance, but as an important factor in the English Renaissance of the sixteenth century.

The textbooks do not answer the important questions. The questions we want answered arise out of our heightened awareness of our own problems. When did poets first begin to take themselves seriously?

When did poets begin to worry about their public, about appreciation and understanding, as well as mere fame? When did the idea of contemporaneity first turn up? Which poets were contemporary poets in our sense? When did poets start to have the weight of the world on their shoulders? When did poets first begin to define poetry, to have a clear notion of what they were driving at? When did they first feel the need to grapple with their age, to record its special sensibility? These questions all add up to an implied portrait of modern poetry, and they can certainly be answered, but not easily, and not in the formal diagrams of official literary history. Our feeling that this age is unique and its problems peculiar to our time can be shown to be a part of the recurrent adolescence, the recurrent growing pains of poetical history. In fact, our acute awareness of public hostility to the current mode demands a study of the origins and mechanism of poetical sales-resistance.

The complex origins of modern English poetry, its mingling of native sources and the foreign stimulus of, say, Baudelaire, Mallarmé, Laforgue and Corbière, its experiments and false starts, its extravagances and excesses, and its settling down in the wake of one pioneer who dominates all followers and all rebels against his rule—and we *must* regard Mr. Eliot as being this pioneer—this very pattern of modern poetry has an almost exact historical parallel. Although 'New Poetry' has turned up at various times, and at increasing speed in the past hundred and fifty years, there has only once been a poet hailed as 'The New Poet', announced and finally accepted as such by his generation, and that was Edmund Spenser, and he may well be taken as the type of the Modern Poet, in our modern conception of him. He was the starting-point of more than two hundred years of poetry, he was the mouthpiece of a generation and an epoch, he paid homage to native tradition in Chaucer, and he was aware of the rôle of the poet as worked out in Italy and in France. Ariosto was his Baudelaire, and Ronsard his Laforgue. He was a live modern experimenter in the technique of verse, its rhythm, its stresses, its music and its imagery. He was aware of the problems of poetic diction and of contemporary speech. He is the perpetual instructor of English poetry in the handling of movement and texture, and in the psychological, the philosophical, the allegorical and the descriptive content of poetry. He was, after Chaucer, our earliest professional poet, though both never lost their amateur status. He taught all our greatest poets, Marlowe, Shakespeare, Milton, Dryden, Pope and Keats, and he is still teaching them:

> Sweet Thames, run softly till I end my song,
> Sweet Thames, run softly, for I speak not loud or
> long.

I dwell on Spenser rather than Chaucer, because Chaucer's main effect is posthumous. There is no record that in his lifetime he was known to be tackling the poetical problems of his age, or that his solutions interested his contemporaries.

Of the immense activity between Chaucer and Spenser we know nothing, alas! Our evidence is all internal evidence. The struggles from which Lydgate

and Dunbar and Wyatt and Surrey emerged must
have been titanic. The process has vanished, and we
must remain content with the results. That the
process included the absorbing of Dante and Boccaccio,
of Petrarch and Seneca, makes us gasp at our ignorance.
Mr. Eliot in his magnificent essay on 'Seneca in
Elizabethan translation' has done much to recreate
the latter part of the process, in the course of which
blank verse emerged. As he says, 'Few things that
can happen to a nation are more important than
the invention of a new form of verse.' Unfortu-
nately that vital portion of our national history is
missing.

It is now thirty-six years since *The Love Song of J.
Alfred Prufrock* was printed, and we think that much has
happened since then, but thirty-six years either side
of 1600 would show us infinitely greater speed of
change, and infinitely fiercer discussion of the nature of
poetry, its scope and technique. Before 1600, Sidney's
Apology for Poetry, Puttenham's *Art of Poetry*, and
Gascoigne's *Notes of Instruction concerning the making of verse
or ryme in English* are only the visible peaks of the ice-
berg. By the 1590's there was a seething battle about
poetry in Spenser, Marlowe and Shakespeare, with
Donne's practice and Chapman's theory to add a new
thrill. After 1600 there was the 'case' of Donne and
the New Poetry, Metaphysical poetry. What do we
know of public taste at this time? It is here that we
get the first big cleavage between the advanced poet
and the general public, with the existence of a highbrow
public for special kinds of tough verse, an arrogant
attitude on the part of the professional poet, and a

reactionary attitude from the general reader and his critical representatives. Francis Beaumont speaks of those 'subtle gallants' who like 'nought that may be understood'. Ben Jonson, apostle of clarity and perspicuity and correctness, wrote in his commonplace book that 'now nothing is good that is natural. . . . That which is writhed and tortured is counted the more exquisite. . . . Nothing is fashionable till it be deform'd; and this is to write like a gentleman'. As early as 1595 George Chapman recognised a special audience for difficult poetry: 'The profane multitude I hate, and only consecrate my strange poems to those searching spirits, whom learning hath made noble.' He speaks of 'the philosophical conceits that my new pen so seriously courteth', and he issues the earliest charter of obscurity:

'Obscurity in affection of words, and indigested conceits, is pedantical and childish; but where it shroudeth itself in the heart of his subject, uttered with fitness of figure, and expressive epithets; with that darkness will I still labour to be shadowed.'

Even Dr. Johnson supports this view when he writes that 'words are only hard to those who do not understand them, and the critic ought always to enquire, whether he is incommoded by the fault of the writer, or by his own. Every author does not write for every reader'.

The new taste was for what the new jargon called 'strong lines', metaphysical images and conceits, practised by the poets, praised and appraised by fellow travellers, and attacked by those to whom modern poetry is always a personal affront.

'These slight flashes of ungrounded fancy (ingenious nothings and mere embroideries upon cobwebs) that the world swarms with . . . are only laboured for and attended to because they take best, and most please the corrupt taste and false appetite of the sordid and barbarous times we live in.'   The tune is very familiar. It is the battle-march of the Philistine cohorts. The middle-brow position is represented by Drummond of Hawthornden.   Poetry, he says,
'subsisteth by herself, and after one demeanour and continuance, her beauty appeareth to all ages.   In vain have some men of late, transformers of everything, consulted upon her reformation, and endeavoured to abstract her to metaphysical ideas and scholastical quiddities, denuding her of her own habits and those ornaments with which she hath amused the world some thousand years. . . . Neither do I think that a good piece of poetry which Homer, Virgil, Ovid, Petrarch . . . and Ronsard, if they were alive and had that language, could not understand, and reach the sense of the writer.'

Contemporary poetry, we can see from this, is already a contemporary problem, and the age participates publicly in the struggle.   The public is conscious of what is going on, and the poets are aware of what has been achieved.   The elegies on the death of John Donne, and particularly Thomas Carew's elegy, provide an obituary stocktaking:

> The Muses' garden, with pedantic weeds
> O'erspread, was purg'd by thee; the lazy seeds
> Of servile imitation thrown away,
> And fresh invention planted; . . .

Thou hast redeem'd, and open'd us a mine
Of rich and pregnant fancy; drawn a line
Of masculine expression, . . .

     to the awe of thy imperious wit
Our stubborn language bends, made only fit
With her tough, thick-ribb'd hoops to gird about
Thy giant fancy, which had prov'd too stout
For their soft melting phrases. . . .

But thou art gone, and thy strict laws will be
Too hard for libertines in poetry.
They will repeal the goodly exil'd train
Of gods and goddesses, which in thy just reign
Were banish'd nobler poems; now, with these,
The silenc'd tales o' th' *Metamorphoses*
Shall stuff their lines, and swell the windy page,
Till verse, refin'd by thee, in this last age
Turn ballad-rhyme, or those old idols be
Ador'd again with new apostacy.

The march of poetry can be measured only if we
have a common measure, and it is not often that we
find a critic who confesses to his changes of taste, and
is prepared to recant. We have such a measure in
John Dryden, who is not only a great critic, but a
sensitive barometer of taste. Fifty years of inner
poetical history is reflected in his critical writing and
in his poetical practice. We watch the decline of the
Metaphysicals, the eclipse of Donne and later of
Cowley, 'the darling of my youth, the famous Cowley'.
We watch new 'old masters' emerging, wearing the
new look, 'nothing so even, sweet and flowing as Mr.
Waller, nothing so majestic, so correct as Sir John
Denham', so he writes in 1668. John Dennis, who

later had no use for Alexander Pope, marks their passing. 'Suckling', he writes to Dryden in 1694, 'Suckling, Cowley and Denham, who formerly ravish'd me in every part of them, now appear tasteless to me in most, and Waller himself, with all his gallantry, and all that admirable art of his turns, appears three quarters prose to me.' A new god was emerging, above the battle almost, to join the other gods, Homer and Virgil, in their sublimity—Milton. Dryden did more to establish Milton as a factor in English poetry than any other critic of his time, and it is a revealing fact in the history of taste that Jacob Tonson the publisher confessed that he had made more money out of *Paradise Lost* than out of any other poem.

Our consumer's history of poetry still lacks an important guide to contemporary feeling. The Press had not yet emerged. It was born as Dryden died, and from the eighteenth century onwards the reviews both reveal and obscure the march of poetry. Reviewing is valuable because it gives, when it wishes, chapter and verse. The charming habit of filling space by quotation instead of comment is one from which we profit largely. It is from the critical reviews that we learn, in the struggle round Gray's *Odes*, of the new factors entering poetry, the new notions of sublimity, of originality, of the primitive, and of yet another interpretation of 'nature', positively the last, it is declared. And suddenly, at the turn of the century, poetry becomes serious again, and the poets become serious about themselves and their function. Wordsworth announces that a poet is a special kind of person, 'with more lively sensibility' than other men,

whose 'spontaneous overflow of powerful feelings'
must compel other men's attention. He announces,
too, a change of subject-matter, ranging from simple
man and raw nature to 'the remotest discoveries of
the Chemist, the Botanist, or Mineralogist'. Discussion
becomes fierce and universal, and even vicious. The
Edinburgh Review in 1807 quotes from Wordsworth's
Ode to Duty,

> Thou dost preserve the stars from wrong;
> And the most ancient heavens, through Thee, are
>   fresh and strong.

and comments, 'the last two lines seem to be utterly
without meaning'. Of the *Ode on the Intimations of
Immortality* it says: 'This is beyond doubt the most
illegible and unintelligible part of the publication.
We can pretend to give no analysis or explanation of it;
our readers must make what they can of the following
extracts:

> Whither is fled the visionary gleam?
> Where is it now, the glory and the dream.

and

> High instincts before which our mortal Nature
> Did tremble like a guilty Thing surprised.'

The critic was baffled completely by

> My heart leaps up when I behold
> A rainbow in the sky.

Coleridge's *Christabel* is labelled a 'rhapsody of
delirium', *The Ancient Mariner* 'a Dutch attempt at
German sublimity'. Of Shelley's *Adonais* one verdict
is that 'its poetry is contemptible, a mere collection

of bloated words heaped on each other without order, harmony or meaning '. *The Cenci* is 'the production of a fiend, and calculated for the entertainment of devils in Hell. A dish of carrion seasoned with sulphur as a spice'. From *Prometheus Unbound* the critics choose specimens of Shelley's 'villainous compounds'. 'The Babylonish jargon which is found in every wearisome page of this tissue of insufferable buffoonery.' And yet, alongside of this, there were the poets' contributions to the debate: Keats's *Letters*, Coleridge's *Biographia Literaria*, and Shelley's *Defence of Poetry*.

I do not put these things forward as mere curiosities, but as documents in the history of sales-resistance. In them we can find parallels to our own day's rejection of pylons and gasometers, of sparking plugs and arterial roads, in poetry. It is necessary to know precisely what contemporaries found startling or new, what exactly the nineteenth century found to boggle at in Swinburne, for instance. The *Saturday Review* informs us that 'With Mr. Swinburne's *Atalanta* came in the constant use of "iron", the eternal reference to "fire" and "blood", and a certain meteoric way of writing about the great blind forces of the world, stars, winds, foam and so forth. . . . Before Mr. Swinburne we almost doubt whether girls were called "white", or necks and other portions of the human frame "warm"; certainly kisses did not "sting"; nor were things in general apt to be so "wet".' It is just as important to know this as to learn of the shock of Coleridge's

> As idle as a painted ship
> Upon a painted ocean

or of Mr. Eliot's

> When the evening is spread out against the sky
> Like a patient etherized upon a table.

Poetry must always be renewed, and it is the renewal which is always an affront to a public conditioned with difficulty to a previous phase. Shelley put his finger on the essential nature of this process of renewal when he wrote that the language of poetry 'is vitally metaphorical; that is, it marks the before unapprehended relations of things and perpetuates their apprehension, until words, which represent them, become, through time, signs for portions or classes of thought, instead of pictures of integral thoughts; and then, if no new poets should arise to create afresh the associations which have been thus disorganised, language will be dead to all the nobler purposes of human intercourse.' Which is as much as to say that new poetry with a new and direct approach to life is essential if mankind is to remain alert.

Thirty-six years ago the struggle began afresh. D. H. Lawrence affirmed that 'the essence of poetry with us in this age of stark and unlovely actualities is a stark directness, without a shadow of a lie, or a shadow of deflection anywhere. Everything can go, but this stark, bare, rocky directness of statement, this alone makes poetry to-day'; and with such affirmations the story begins again.

The *Quarterly Review*, nearly one hundred years after its attack on Keats, gets busy again. The old jokes are given a new turn. Instead of saying that *Prometheus Unbound* is rightly named, because nobody would think of binding it, it quotes with approval Ezra Pound's line 'I am half-cracked'. It fulminates against 'the unmetrical, incoherent banalities of these literary Cubists', and it quotes in horror, for the first time in modern criticism, the lines:

> I grow old . . . I grow old. . . .
> I shall wear the bottoms of my trousers rolled.
>
> Shall I part my hair behind? Do I dare to eat
>   a peach?
> I shall wear white flannel trousers, and walk upon
>   the beach.
> I have heard the mermaids singing, each to each.
> I do not think that they will sing to me.[1]

The process has repeated itself in a modern setting. Poetical history has come full circle, and the contemporary observer, with wisdom before the event, sadly anticipates the verdict of the scholar. It is no accident, I think, that the volume, the *Catholic Anthology* of 1915, in which Mr. Eliot's *Prufrock* first appeared in England, should have been prefaced by W. B. Yeats's poem *The Scholars*:[2]

> Bald heads forgetful of their sins,
> Old, learned, respectable bald heads
> Edit and annotate the lines
> That young men, tossing on their beds,
> Rhymed out in love's despair
> To flatter beauty's ignorant ear.
>
> They'll cough in the ink to the world's end;
> Wear out the carpet with their shoes
> Earning respect; have no strange friend;
> If they have sinned nobody knows.
> Lord, what would they say
> Should their Catullus walk that way?

1. Copyright 1936, by T. S. Eliot
2. Copyright 1950, by The Macmillan Company

II

What is Modernity?

WHAT is modernity? What indeed! If we could
answer this, if we could say what posterity will find to
be the specific essence of our time, we should be
prophets. But my question is somewhat less com-
prehensive. What is that peculiar note of our time
which we recognise and instinctively love or hate
when we find it in poetry? What is the special quality of
modern poetry? Is it obscurity, is it private reference,
is it cacophony, is it the immediate and not the eternal,
the particular and not the general? Is it the personal
and satiric note? Is it the anti-heroic and debunking?
Is it all or some of these? The problem is not so
simple. There are contradictions. There is pure
poetry and there is impure poetry, social and political
poetry. In texture modern poetry is a poetry of
nuances. In structure it is a balance of tensions and
conflicts. At its worst it is a cluster of disorganised
and incoherent fragments; at its best it is a dome of
many-coloured glass, staining the white radiance of
eternity.

There are three questions we must ask ourselves.
Are these the qualities of modern poetry? are they
exclusively modern? and if they are not, what is their
history? Let us look at the notion of 'pure poetry'.
This notion has come to us in two waves. The first
wave is a romantic notion, and belongs to the Pre-

Romantic age of the middle of the eighteenth century, when poetry was sought in primitive poetry, in ancient poetry, in ballads and in archaic writing, much as modern art sought its inspiration in archaic sculpture and African carvings. The second wave is in the Symbolist movement of the end of the nineteenth century. If we like to attach names to the two waves, we can call them Ossian and Mallarmé. In both there is a striving beyond mere statement in order to gain a special effect. The earlier movement was a movement *against* something. The later was a movement *towards* something, and only incidentally against the moral and the didactic in poetry.

Poetry is made of comparisons, simple or complex, open or concealed. The richness of poetry is obtained by mixing or interweaving or juxtaposing these comparisons. The mixture is either a mechanical mixture or a chemical mixture: when the mechanical becomes chemical the explosion takes place. That is the difference between prose and poetry. In prose all comparisons are simple and uncompounded. In poetry all metaphors are mixed metaphors. They are not always so naked and unashamedly mixed as in Shakespeare's *Hamlet*:

> to suffer
> The slings and arrows of outrageous fortune,
> Or to take arms against a sea of troubles. . . .

or as in *Macbeth*:

> Was the hope drunk
> Wherein you dress'd yourself? hath it slept since?
> And wakes it now, to look so green and pale
> At what it did so freely?

Poetry has always striven to be something other than prose. Wordsworth and Coleridge had their strong views on the border-line between the two. Modern poetry is facing the same problem by taking speech, when it is the language of men in a state of excitement, and making certain that that excitement lifts it above prose. There is a danger that the excitement may not be communicated. Wordsworth's contemporaries were not yet attuned, and often thought his verse prose. ₊ In the bar-room scene of Mr. Eliot's *The Waste Land* the prosaic conversation is fitted into the larger cadences of the epic:

> HURRY UP PLEASE ITS TIME
> HURRY UP PLEASE ITS TIME
> Goonight Bill. Goonight Lou. Goonight May.
>   Goonight.
> Ta ta. Goonight. Goonight.
> Good night, ladies, good night, sweet ladies, good
>   night, good night.

This is one kind of modernity.

The first wave of pure poetry led to the first Romantic movement, with its pioneers in Wordsworth and Coleridge, its culmination in Keats and Shelley, and its decadence in Tennyson. The second wave led to the second Romantic movement, known more widely as the Symbolist movement, with its climax in Mallarmé and Valéry, and its decadence in all those poets, in France, Germany, England, and America who follow in Mallarmé's wake: Rilke, Stefan George, Eliot, Yeats. It is this decadence which is the modernity of to-day. Both waves are intimately linked. Leigh Hunt, when he reviewed Keats's first book of poems,

* From *Collected Poems 1909–1935* by T. S. Eliot, copyright 1936, by Harcourt, Brace and Company, Inc.

said that Keats wrote 'poetry for poetry's sake'. The Symbolist movement is built on the notion of ' art for art's sake' as spread by Théophile Gautier.

The story of this second wave gives us a fascinating glimpse of the process of poetry. It all goes back to Edgar Allan Poe, a poet admittedly not of the first rank, but a phenomenon of the profoundest significance for modern European poetry. In Europe it started with Baudelaire, who decided to use Poe as a projection of his own very special views and feelings about literature. He found, in Poe's critical and other writings, things which seemed like his own secretly formulated notions. In Poe's *The Poetic Principle* he found the doctrine of 'pure poetry' as against the moral and the didactic, and in *The Philosophy of Composition* found the idea of conscious poetic manipulation as opposed to poetic inspiration. Théophile Gautier, in a preface to Baudelaire's *Les Fleurs du Mal*, expanded these views and added an insistence on the musical value of poetry, on pure sculptured form, and on the notion of correspondences between the senses, developed on the basis of Baudelaire's 'Les parfums, les couleurs et les sons se confondent'.

Verlaine, too, echoes statements of Poe which he could never have read, and his poetry and that of Rimbaud are the fruit of a long and strange process of misinterpretation and creative misunderstanding. Rimbaud's *Le Bateau Ivre*, though never concretely inspired by Poe, could not have been written without the absorption, in the French literature before him, of Poe's hallucinations. One line in Rimbaud, in which he talks of a 'Maelstrom', betrays him to anyone who was ever steeped, as we all were steeped, in Poe's *Tales of Mystery and Imagination*. Literary history has neglected this process of misinterpretation and misunderstanding. We need to investigate, not the dreary chains of influence where we can show that one writer copied another in literal detail, but the more fascinating chains which link one poet to another he has never read but only read about or heard about, whose ideas vaguely apprehended or even misapprehended serve as catalytic agents for his own development. Such was the function of Edgar Allan Poe in the cat's-cradle of modern poetic influences.

The culmination of this strange influence of Poe came with Stephane Mallarmé, and with him a method, far from Poe's, which is our own method. To understand this we must go back to Poe's æsthetic doctrine. Poe speaks of 'a suggestive indefiniteness' as an essential ingredient of true musical poetry, but there is one critical comment of his which I think has never been fitted into its place in the story. It comes in a review of Thomas Moore's poetry which I feel sure none of the French poets had ever read, and it makes Poe's indirect influence all the more important and uncanny. He suggests that the distinction between the fancy and the imagination in poetry lies in what he calls the mystical, and he is rather proud of the idea. 'The term *mystic*,' he says, 'is here employed in the sense of Schlegel and of most other German critics. It is applied by them to that class of composition in which there lies beneath the transparent upper current of meaning an under or *suggestive* one. What we vaguely term the *moral* of any sentiment is its mystic or secondary expression. It has the vast force of an accompaniment in music.'

That is the secret of this great shift in poetic feeling, music. Poe, himself a confluence of the great rivers of criticism flowing from Coleridge and from German Romanticism, is responsible in modern Europe for that double fusion, the fusion of the senses and the fusion of the arts. The Romantics declared that 'architecture is frozen music', and later in the middle of the nineteenth century Walter Pater as a critic, Swinburne and Baudelaire as poets, proclaimed that 'all the arts aspire to a condition of music'. Whatever the origin of the idea, and whatever the meaning of mystic may be, Poe has hit on the essential nature of modern poetry—the suggestive overtones and undertones of implication which lie parallel with the surface meaning. Here, with the suggestive indefiniteness, and the conscious craftsmanship, is the whole method of Mallarmé to which all our modern poets are indebted directly or indirectly.

The story now brings us back to England. Among the frequenters of Mallarmé's famous salon in the Rue de Rome was Arthur Symons, a fine and unjustly forgotten critic. In 1899 he wrote his book on *The Symbolist Movement in Literature*, forgotten and no longer necessary, but in its time epoch-making. He dedicated it to W. B. Yeats, as 'the chief representative of that movement' in England. Yeats also visited Mallarmé, but his French was not good enough to profit directly from him, and he admits the influence on himself of Symons's translations from Mallarmé. In 1899 the book was perhaps premature, but Symons did drop a tiny pebble in the ocean. He wrote of Verlaine and of Rimbaud, and gave a prophetic analysis of Jules Laforgue, and described the method and theory of Stephane Mallarmé. Unknowingly it is Poe's theory of suggestive indefiniteness and musical overtones. Mallarmé's own doctrine of vagueness is very explicit. 'To name an object,' he says, 'is to do away with three-quarters of that delight in a poem which consists in unravelling it bit by bit. It must be suggested. Poetry must always remain a riddle.' And Paul Valéry, his disciple, when he was elected to the French Academy, echoed him. 'Certain poets,' he said, 'insist that the mind shall work for its pleasures. They propound riddles to us.'

Arthur Symons was close enough to Mallarmé to be able to describe this method of writing. Nothing like it had ever been put down for poets to read; and this is what he says:

Mallarmé has received a mental sensation. 'This sensation begins to form in his brain, at first probably no more than a rhythm, absolutely without words. Gradually thought begins to concentrate itself . . . upon the sensation, already struggling to find its own consciousness. Delicately, stealthily, with infinitely timid precaution, words present themselves, at first in silence. Every word seems like a desecration, seems, the clearer it is, to throw back the original sensation farther and farther into the darkness. But, guided always by the rhythm, which is the executive soul, . . . words come slowly, one by one, shaping the message. Imagine the poem already written down, at least composed. In its very imperfection, it is clear, it shows the

links by which it has been riveted together; the whole
process of its construction can be studied.'

So far this is subtle description, but as a process it is
nothing out of the ordinary, and Symons goes on to
describe Mallarmé's special contribution:

'Now most writers would be content; but with
Mallarmé the work has only begun. In the final
result there must be no sign of the making, there must
be only the thing made. He works over it, word by
word, changing a word here, for its colour, which is not
precisely the colour required, a word there, for the
break it makes in the music. A new image occurs to
him, rarer, subtler, than the one he has used; the
image is transferred.

'By the time the poem has reached, as it seems to
him, a flawless unity, the steps of the progress have
been only too effectually effaced; and while the poet,
who has seen the thing from the beginning, still sees
the relation of point to point, the reader, who comes
to it only in its final stage, finds himself in a not un-
natural bewilderment. Pursue this manner of writing
to its ultimate development; start with an enigma,
and then withdraw the key of the enigma; and you
arrive, easily, at the frozen impenetrability of those
latest sonnets, in which the absence of all punctuation
is scarcely a recognisable hindrance.'

This may not have been one hundred per cent.
Mallarmé's method. Mallarmé may even have denied
it completely, though I doubt it. It may not have
been Mallarmé's method, but it was *a* method, and
the *rumour* of it (even without a confirmatory reading
of Mallarmé's poems, and even with such reading but

without full understanding) started English poets on a new line.

In 1899 English poetry was not ready for Symons's book. In 1908, on its second edition, the poetic world had caught up with him. Mr. Eliot wrote: 'I owe Mr. Symons a great debt. But for having read his book I should not, in the year 1908, have heard of Laforgue and Rimbaud; I should probably not have begun to read Verlaine; and but for reading Verlaine, I should not have heard of Corbière. So the Symons book is one of those which have affected the course of my life.' Arthur Symons's description of Laforgue's poetry, with its 'subtle use of colloquialisms, slang, neologism, technical terms for their allusive, their reflected meanings—the *vers libre* which is at the same time correct verse, the acute consciousness of daily life, which cannot omit, mentally, a single hour of the day', and above all, 'the possibilities for art which come from the sickly modern being, with his clothes, his nerves: the mere fact that he flowers from the soil of his epoch', all this in 1899 is a prophetic description of the early poems of Mr. T. S. Eliot.

From Laforgue comes this new Werther, this René, this Hamlet, this Prufrock, which is the latest in a long list of those who have flowered from the soil of their epoch. Hamlet is another of those figures which must be taken out of their chronological epoch. Hamlet was born again in the Romantic age of Coleridge and Goethe, after his first incarnation as the 'Melancholy Man' of the Elizabethan age. Laforgue was much concerned with Hamlet, and when Prufrock says he is *not* Prince Hamlet he gives himself away.

The impact of a poet's epoch on his poetry is a fascinating study. We scrutinise Shakespeare to establish his experience. We examine Mr. Auden to record the progress of his alertness and our limping march after him. It is sometimes amusing to reverse the process, to see what the poet does for his epoch. The other day I stumbled by chance on two allusions to Magna Carta. I am interested in the 'myth' of Magna Carta as it has been called, but when I turn to the historians they tell me only of externals. I prefer the evidence of the poets. Shakespeare writes a play about King John in which he fails even to mention Runnymede and Magna Carta. Thirty years later Ben Jonson writes a comedy and makes a kind of music-hall joke of it, as if it were a new racket. Towards the end of the seventeenth century Dryden, in speaking of certain poetical devices, can say easily and proudly, 'I regard them now as the Magna Carta of heroic poetry, and am too much an Englishman to lose what my ancestors have gained for me'. Here is the history of the myth of Magna Carta in three nutshells, one of them empty. It is a characteristic of modern poetry that an allusion to Magna Carta is as much in place as an allusion to Kafka or Freud, to Cupid or Alexander the Great.

Symbolism has been defined by Mr. Edmund Wilson, not very convincingly, as 'an attempt, through complicated association of ideas, represented by a medley of metaphors, to communicate unique personal feelings'. I take exception to this: a *medley* of metaphors is a very unfair and inaccurate label. For 'communicate' I would substitute 'offer', and for 'unique personal

feelings' I would suggest 'facets of contemporary
sensibility', so that the amended definition might run:
'Symbolism is an attempt, through a subtly articulated
pattern of metaphors, to offer some facets of contemporary sensibility.' I say 'offer' because the
problem of communication is the crucial problem of
modern poetry: communication and obscurity. Mr.
Eliot says that 'genuine poetry can communicate before
it is understood'. Isaac Rosenberg spoke of poetry
that is 'understandable and still ungraspable'. Unique
personality, too, is something of a myth. Shelley
wrote of the community of poets sharing the same
epoch, or, as we should say, the same sensibility.
Shakespeare was almost morbidly aware of his exact
contemporary Marlowe, as he was of his younger
contemporaries Beaumont and Fletcher. Eliot and
Pound acted upon each other. Eliot and Auden are
not unaware of each other. The sum total of contemporary sensibility is made up of all the facets the
far-from-unique poets offer. 'The Poets,' said Shelley
in one of his fine images, 'are the mirrors of the gigantic
shadows which futurity casts upon the present.'

How is this contemporary sensibility recorded and
preserved for futurity? It can be recorded by the
critic or by the poet. Remy de Gourmont has been
described as the critical consciousness of a generation,
as supplying the conscious formulæ of a sensibility in
process of formation. To Remy de Gourmont French
Symbolist poetry and English modern poetry owe a
vast debt for recording the growth of contemporary
sensibility. 'Style,' he said, 'is a specialisation of
sensibility.' The poet can record it in two ways,

through rhythm, or through imagery. 'A man who devises new rhythms,' it has been said, 'is a man who extends and refines our sensibility.'

It is, however, mainly through imagery that the modern poet at all times pays his fees of citizenship. In our own day, it is the special imagery of the Metaphysical poets that has worked most powerfully. It was a right instinct which turned the attention of an age grappling with overwhelming scientific problems, to a similar age staggering under a similar burden. We must not forget that the Romantic age, too, had its scientific problems. Priestley and Sir Humphry Davy were very close to the poets, and Shelley's footnotes to *Queen Mab* are just as startling as those to *The Waste Land* or Mr. Auden's *New Year Letter*. The point about the Metaphysicals which is important is, to quote once more, that 'they had a mechanism of sensibility which could devour any experience'. And in our half-way house it is fascinating to notice that Théophile Gautier's preface to Baudelaire's *Les Fleurs du Mal* contains an accurate description of the essential metaphysical process of imagery, and of the process of modern imagery—the secret and invisible welding of the most contradictory elements, combined with that confusion of the senses, or rather fusion of the senses, which is the hall-mark of modern suggestive writing. Ossian started it, Wordsworth continued it, Shelley perfected it. Poe did propaganda for it. Mallarmé gave it new life. Valéry put seven veils round it, and every modern poet plays with it in his nursery. In the fourth act of Shelley's *Prometheus Unbound* lie models for every modern Symbolist poet.

Listen too,
How every pause is filled with under-notes,
Clear, silver, icy, keen, awakening tones,
Which pierce the sense, and live within the soul,
As the sharp stars pierce winter's crystal air
And gaze upon themselves within the sea.

And never, I think, has the interfusion of the senses
been more grandly shown than in the following
passage:

And from the other opening in the wood
Rushes, with loud and whirlwind harmony,
A sphere, which is as many thousand spheres,
Solid as crystal, yet through all its mass
Flow, as through empty space, music and light:
Ten thousand orbs involving and involved,
Purple and azure, white, and green, and golden,
Sphere within sphere; and every space between
Peopled with unimaginable shapes,
Such as ghosts dream dwell in the lampless deep,
Yet each inter-transpicuous, and they whirl
Over each other with a thousand motions,
Upon a thousand sightless axles spinning,
And with the force of self-destroying swiftness,
Intensely, slowly, solemnly roll on,
Kindling with mingled sounds, and many tones,
Intelligible words and music wild.
With mighty whirl the multitudinous orb
Grinds the bright brook into an azure mist
Of elemental subtlety, like light;
And the wild odour of the forest flowers,
The music of the living grass and air,
The emerald light of leaf-entangled beams
Round its intense yet self-conflicting speed,
Seem kneaded into one aëreal mass
Which drowns the sense.

Transfer this from the outer spheres to the present earth, and wrap this technique round the skeleton of contemporary sensibility, by way of Poe and Baudelaire, Gautier, Verlaine, and Mallarmé, and we have modern poetry.

III

The Coming of the Image

THE Imagists are a neglected school, more talked about than read, and indeed they are not easy to read because they have been squeezed out of all the popular and influential anthologies where their fertilising power might be felt, and their collected volumes, in which they do not appear to such good advantage, are scarce or out of print. Only Harold Monro, with his heart among the Georgians, was lover of poetry enough and generous enough to turn at least his head in their direction. Imagism is a faded legend and its history has been misrepresented by interested parties. Let me try to give a true picture.

The movement began forty years ago, in 1908, when T. E. Hulme founded a Poets' Club which met in Soho every Wednesday to dine and to read poetry. A small pamphlet was issued *For Christmas 1908* which contained Hulme's *Autumn*, the first and most famous of the Imagist poems. This is the poem:

> A touch of cold in the Autumn night
> I walked abroad,
> And saw the ruddy moon lean over a hedge,
> Like a red-faced farmer.
> I did not stop to speak, but nodded;
> And round about were the wistful stars
> With white faces like town children.

Another member of the club was Edward Storer, who
issued a volume of poems called *Mirrors of Illusion*.
It bears no date, but the British Museum copy is
stamped 11th January 1909, so we may reasonably
assume that it was published by the end of 1908. It
includes one poem entitled *Image*. Here is the whole
poem:

> Forsaken lovers,
> Burning to a chaste white moon,
> Upon strange pyres of loneliness and drought.

It is the first modern English poem, so far as I know,
to be titled *Image*. Both poems are about the moon,
and it seems as though the history of poetry in all ages is
the attempt to find new images for the moon.

Early in 1909 T. E. Hulme met Mr. F. S. Flint, and
from 25th March a new group was formed consisting of,
or including, Hulme, Storer, Flint, an Irish poet Joseph
Campbell, and Miss Florence Farr. On 22nd April
1909 there was introduced an American poet, Ezra
Pound, who had published his volume of *Personæ* six
days before. Pound read them his *Sestina: Altaforte*,
a mixture of Browning and Provençal poetry, and it is
recorded that the café trembled.

The early historian of the movement is Mr. F. S.
Flint, and his short history of Imagism appeared in
the special Imagist number of *The Egoist* on 1st May
1915. Mr. Flint recalls that there was 'a lot of talk
and practice among us, Storer leading it chiefly, of
what we called "The Image". We were very much
influenced by modern French Symbolist poetry'.
Of Ezra Pound's rôle he tells us that 'he could not be

made to believe that there was any French poetry
after Ronsard. He was very full of his troubadours;
but I do not remember (says Mr. Flint) that he did
more than attempt to illustrate (or refute) our theories
occasionally with their example'; and he says more
categorically, in a letter to Mr. Richard Aldington,
'that Pound added *nothing* to their meetings—absolutely
nothing'. Pound's ignorance of the Symbolists was
to be remedied, through Mr. Flint in 1912 and Mr.
John Gould Fletcher in 1913. In November 1909
Mr. Flint published a volume *In the Net of the Stars*,
containing a poem called *A Mood and its Images*, and
for Christmas 1909 appeared *The Book of the Poets' Club*,
by a group of writers of whom the best known names
to-day are T. E. Hulme, Ezra Pound and Hannen
Swaffer. It contained Hulme's two poems *The Embankment* and *The Conversation*; and so ended the first
phase, the softer phase, the '90'ish phase of the 'School
of the Image'.

The next phase is the invention of the label 'Imagist'
and the reign of Ezra Pound. It coincides with the
beginning of the Great Poetry Boom which lasted from
1912 to 1922 and during which more than 1000 poets
published more than 2000 volumes between them.
It was the time of Harold Monro's *Poetry Review*, of
'The Poetry Bookshop' with its Georgian anthologies
and its Poetry Readings in the loft in Devonshire Street,
of the founding of the Chicago magazine *Poetry* in 1912,
of the Imagist anthologies, of Alfred Kreymborg's
Others, of Miss Edith Sitwell's *Wheels*, of *Oxford Poetry*,
of *Coterie*, of *Blast* and *The Little Review*.

Ezra Pound became the impresario of the Imagist

movement. He supplied the name, he found the poets, he sought out the white hopes, he groomed them, he taught them, he put them through their paces. The present holder of the world heavy-weight championship, Mr. T. S. Eliot, is very grateful to his old trainer. He allowed him to blue-pencil *The Waste Land*. His reputation was such that the previous champion, W. B. Yeats, from a different stable, wrote in 1924 that 'some seven or eight years ago I asked my friend Ezra Pound to point out everything in the language of my poems he thought an abstraction, and I learned from him how much farther the movement against abstraction had gone than my generation had thought possible'.

Why is Ezra Pound such an important figure in the development of modern English poetry? Because he was a busybody, a meddler, a thruster, a contact-man of the arts. He appointed himself foreign editor of *Poetry* in 1912, helped to get material for *The Egoist* in 1914, was European editor of *The Little Review* in 1917. He supplied America with the poems of H. D., and of Richard Aldington, the first of the new group to be labelled 'Imagist'. He invented the word 'Imagist' for the poems of T. E. Hulme, whose complete poetical works of five tiny poems he published as an appendix to his own *Ripostes* in 1912, and in season and out he preached the doctrine of poetry as an art and a craft. It was Ezra Pound's doctrine, whatever label he put on it, whatever group he attached himself to, and adopted and dominated. In Harold Monro's *Poetry Review* in February 1912 we find his Credo. There is no word of Image or Imagism in it, but the doctrine is there, the belief in technique, the belief in absolute rhythm, that rhythm 'which corresponds exactly to the emotion or shade of emotion to be expressed', in the mastery of all known forms and systems of metres, the insistence on precision, the avoidance of convention and *cliché*, of rhetoric and inversions. And above all that doctrine of hardness which distinguishes the work of the best Imagist poets. This is how his Credo concludes:

'As to Twentieth century poetry, the poetry which I expect to see written during the next decade or so, it will, I think, move against poppy-cock, it will be harder and saner, it will be . . . "nearer the bone". It will be as much like granite as it can be, its force will lie in its truth . . . it will not try to seem forcible by rhetorical din, and luxurious riot. We will have fewer painted adjectives impeding the shock and stroke of it. At least for myself, I want it so, austere, direct, free from emotional slither.'

For the second number of Chicago *Poetry* in November 1912 Pound had sent three poems by Richard Aldington, described by the editor as 'a young English poet, one of the "Imagistes", a group of ardent Hellenists who are pursuing interesting experiments in *vers libre*; trying to attain in English certain subtleties of cadence of the kind which Mallarmé and his followers have studied in French'. Nearly all the ingredients are adumbrated in this early 'blurb': Hellenism, symbolism, *vers libre* and cadence. Their moment of glory was to come when Remy de Gourmont, as almost the last thing he wrote before his death in 1915, acclaimed them as the descendants of the French Symbolists, in their horror

3

32384

of the *cliché*, their horror of rhetoric and of the grandiose, of the oratorical style of the followers of Victor Hugo in France and, we may add, of the followers of Tennyson in England.   But I anticipate.

It was in March 1913 that F. S. Flint and Ezra Pound laid down, in the pages of the American *Poetry*, the principles of the movement.   'They were not a revolutionary school', they believed in the best traditions of Sappho, Catullus and Villon.   There were three rules:

(1) Direct treatment of the 'thing', whether subjective or objective.
(2) To use absolutely no word that did not contribute to the presentation.
(3) As regarding rhythm: to compose in sequence of the musical phrase, not in sequence of a metronome.

These are the original rules, expanded later by Richard Aldington and Amy Lowell.   Here, too, is Pound's first definition of the Image:

'An "Image" is that which presents an intellectual and emotional complex in an instant of time.   I use the term "complex",' he wrote, 'rather in the technical sense employed by the newer psychologists such as Hart.'

And here, too, is the famous advice which was to affect all serious poets for the next quarter of a century, and which Mr. Eliot says he himself has given to many an aspiring poet, as well as taken himself:

'Let the candidate fill his mind with the finest cadences he can discover, preferably in a foreign

FERNALD LIBRARY
COLBY JUNIOR COLLEGE
NEW LONDON, NEW HAMPSHIRE

language so that the meaning of the words may
be less likely to divert his attention from the movement; *e.g.*, Saxon charms, Hebridean Folk Songs,
the verse of Dante, and the lyrics of Shakespeare
—if he can dissociate the vocabulary from the
cadence.

'Let the neophyte know assonance and alliteration,
rhyme immediate and delayed, simple and polyphonic,
as a musician would expect to know harmony and
counterpoint and all the minutiæ of his craft. No
time is too great to give to these matters or to any one
of them, even if the artist seldom have need of them.'
And he concludes with the wise caution of Duhamel
and Vildrac's treatise on versification: 'Mais d'abord
il faut être un poète'—but you must be a poet to begin
with.

But we are still a long way from the summit of the
movement. In 1908 the thing started. In 1912 it
begins again, and between 1912 and 1915 the activity
is immense. I do not mean merely that a great deal
of poetry was being written, but that things were
happening everywhere, and tributary streams were
rushing to join the great torrent. The Russian Ballet
exploded its colours and its rhythms into the pool.
Post-Impressionism and Cubism and Futurism were
working their way in. 'The Imagists admitted,'
said Mr. Flint, 'that they were contemporaries of the
Post-Impressionists and the Futurists, but they had
nothing in common with these schools.' The post-
symbolist flirtation with the unconscious was
strengthened by the new Psychology. Freud was
already known to some advanced spirits. African

Negro sculpture was having its effect. Mr. Eliot brought back a Gauguin crucifixion from Paris to Harvard. German expressionism made its devious contribution, and while the puzzled reviewers spoke of Futurist and Cubist poetry, Jacob Epstein and Wyndham Lewis launched the Vorticist movement in their periodical *Blast* in July 1914, or rather *they* launched the movement and Ezra Pound invented its name, and with the new label extended his definition of the Image. 'It is a vortex or cluster of fused ideas,' he said, 'and is endowed with energy.' It was a pity Mr. Pound lost interest in the image, for by now, surely, it would have become an atom-bomb!

It is time now, I think, to look at some Imagist poetry, at three Imagist poems.* The first is called *The Waning Moon.*

> And like a dying lady, lean and pale,
> Who totters forth, wrappt in a gauzy veil,
> Out of her chamber, led by the insane
> And feeble wanderings of her fading brain,
> The moon arose up in the murky East,
> A white and shapeless mass.

The second is called *Evening.*

> The chimneys, rank on rank,
> Cut the clear sky;
> The moon,
> With a rag of gauze about her loins
> Poses among them, an awkward Venus—
>
> And here am I looking wantonly at her
> Over the kitchen sink.

* Copyright 1928, by Richard Aldington

The third is called *Morning at the Window*.

> They are rattling breakfast plates in basement
>   kitchens,
> And along the trampled edges of the street
> I am aware of the damp souls of housemaids
> Sprouting despondently at area gates.
>
> The brown waves of fog toss up to me
> Twisted faces from the bottom of the street,
> And tear from a passer-by with muddy skirts
> An aimless smile that hovers in the air
> And vanishes along the level of the roofs.

The first, of course, is by Percy Bysshe Shelley, written a hundred years before the Imagists, the second by Mr. Richard Aldington at the height of the movement, and the third by Mr. T. S. Eliot, written at Oxford in 1915 after the Imagists had become widely known to serious students of poetry. Between them these poems raise the question: is this notion of the Image new? or if it is not new, what is its precise contribution to modern poetry?

Where does a poet find his images? 'Do you mean,' asks the Philistine, 'that the modern poet is so hard up that he has to go out and *look* for images?' (Nobody believes more firmly in the doctrine of inspiration than the Philistine.) Not only the modern poet, but all poets have sought images. Milton read deliberately in order to store his mind with images. Shakespeare picked up images every time he opened a pamphlet on a bookstall. Chaucer, Spenser, Marlowe, Donne, Coleridge, Keats and Shelley, all sought their imagery. They dug in fields and in mines of imagery, mythology, philosophy, geometry, military history, geography, chemistry, the Bible, anthropology, psychology and war. They recognised an image by the most practical method, by conveying or stealing it. Stealing was their homage. They graded images by their usage of them: the explanatory image, the decorative image or conceit, the metaphysical image which called simultaneously on body and mind, on intellect and emotion. They did not despise even life, or the contemporary world.

> Or as the snail, whose tender horns being hit,
> Shrinks backward in his shelly cave with pain,
> And, there all smother'd up, in shade doth sit,
> Long after fearing to creep forth again:
> So at his bloody view her eyes are fled,
> Into the deep dark cabins of her head.

Keats found this in Shakespeare's *Venus and Adonis* and exulted in it.

Poets recognised images and realised their functions long before the critics analysed them. It was not until the second half of the seventeenth century that the critics began to talk of images, of imaging and of imagery. From their formal discussions of metaphor and simile emerged a feeling for what we understand by imagery, the image which shocks, or stirs, or convinces, or probes a nerve, or glows with a wild surmise.

But what is the Imagist's image? To understand this we must turn awhile from Ezra Pound to Hulme the founder and to the later theorists. T. E. Hulme said, 'It is not sufficient to find analogies. It is necessary to find those which add something to each, and give a sense of wonder. The main function of analogy in poetry is to enable one to dwell and linger upon a point of excitement, to achieve the impossible and convert a point into a line.'

Imagism is not the facile presentation of images or pictures; it is hard, clear, unblurred statement, whether it uses metaphor or not. It must be done by means of the chosen 'exact word'. 'The exact word,' says Mr. Aldington, ' does not mean the word which exactly describes the object in itself, it means the exact word which brings the effect of that object before the reader as it presented itself to the poet's mind at the time of writing the poem.' The object is situated in space, as it were, by removing the blurring irrelevances, just as Michelangelo's figures emerged into space by removing the superfluous marble. It is as easy as that. It is this hard sculptural quality which marks off the best Imagist work, even if the tension, the dwelling upon a point of excitement, cannot be maintained for long. We see it in a poem by H. D. (Hilda Doolittle) like *Garden*.

> O wind, rend open the heat,
> cut apart the heat,
> rend it to tatters.
>
> Fruit cannot drop
> through this thick air—
> fruit cannot fall into heat
> that presses up and blunts
> the points of pears
> and rounds the grapes.
>
> Cut the heat—
> plough through it,
> turning it on either side
> of your path.

We see it in the etched precision of F. S. Flint's poem *Eau-Forte*.

> On black bare trees a stale cream moon
> Hangs dead, and sours the unborn buds.
>
> Two gaunt old hacks, knees bent, heads low,
> Tug, tired and spent, an old horse tram.
>
> Damp smoke, rank mist fill the dark square;
> And round the bend six bullocks come.
>
> A hobbling, dirt-grimed drover guides
> Their clattering feet—
> > their clattering feet!
> > > to the slaughterhouse.

But is all this Imagist poetry hard, to the exclusion of emotion? Has it no warmth, no music, no feeling, no sentiment even? The Imagists claimed that their chosen form of free-verse, *vers libre*, by its emancipation from regular rhythm gave a far subtler music to their poetry. They claimed, too, a strong tradition for such verse in English literature: Dryden, Milton's *Samson Agonistes*, Matthew Arnold and W. E. Henley. Henley's *London Voluntaries* influenced the Imagists very strongly. It has not perhaps been noticed that the 'wistful stars' of T. E. Hulme's *Autumn* come from Henley's *Rhymes and Rhythms*. Mr. Flint invented the term 'unrhymed cadences' for some of his own and his friends' poems. He took the idea from the French poets. He called his 1915 volume *Cadences*, as Mr. Richard Aldington called his volume of the same year *Images*. Mr. Eliot in his *Reflections on Vers Libre* in 1917 was pushing an open door, for as early as 1912 Mr.

Flint had admitted that *vers libre* was the most difficult of forms, but had also found a special virtue in the lay-out of poems in short lines, lines which, read correctly, in a kind of typographical punctuation, have a very cunning rhythm. If there is one historical merit which the Imagist movement has earned, it is the proud assertion and proof that 'a cadenced poem is written to be read aloud, in this way only will its rhythm be felt. Poetry is a spoken and not a written art'.

This spoken and carefully cadenced quality is found in Mr. John Rodker's poems of August 1914. He has never had his due as a poet, although he appeared in the Imagist anthologies and the Imagist periodicals. In his poem *Immanence* the controlled free rhythms are emphasised by the typographical disposition.

> Cool   water   pours
> Into   dim   silence.
> Through   the   tense   shade
> The   musk   of   far   roses
> Gloses
> The   sense. . . .
>
> Cool   water   pours . . .
> Dissolving   thin   sleep
> From   the   corners   of   mind. . . .
> But   the   eyes   are   more   blind
> And   the   slumber   more   deep. . . .
>
> The   fierce   heart   o'   the   rose
> Bursts   in   the   sun. . . .
>
> . . . cool . . . water . . . pours.

Among the many sources of Imagist poetry was the

suggestive Japanese form known as the 'stop-short',
because the words stopped and the meaning went on.
The early Imagists wrote hundreds of them. They
are cadences in miniature, and because they are so
tiny I can give three examples. Mr. Aldington's
New Love: [1]

> She has new leaves
> After her dead flowers,
> Like the little almond tree
> Which the frost hurt.

Or Mr. Pound's *Fan-piece, for her Imperial Lord:* [2]

> O fan of white silk,
>   clear as frost on the grass-blade,
> You also are laid aside.

Or his more modern *In a Station of the Metro:* [3]

> The apparition of these faces in the crowd;
> Petals on a wet, black bough.

But I must give the last word to the pioneer, to T. E.
Hulme's *Fantasia of a fallen gentleman on a cold, bitter
night on the Embankment,* published in 1909. I quote it
because Mr. Eliot has praised it for its beauty, and
because of its subtle dance of evasion around the
iambic pentameter.

> Once, in finesse of fiddles found I ecstasy,
> In a flash of gold heels on the hard pavement.
> Now see I
> That warmth's the very stuff of poesy.
> Oh, God, make small
> The old star-eaten blanket of the sky,
> That I may fold it round me and in comfort lie.

1. Copyright by Richard Aldington
2. Copyright 1917, by Ezra Pound
3. Ibid.

The Imagists have much to offer, their conciseness, their exploration of the prose tradition in verse, their hardness, their relevance, their craftsman's conscience, their horror of rhetoric, 'rhetoric—wring its neck!' they echoed from France. With these and their supple and flexible speech, their absence of emotional slither, they had a method ready for a time when the poet might have something to say, and a subtler melody for when he might have something to sing. It is the Imagist ideal, rather than the Imagist practice, which has been so influential. 'In poetry,' said Mr. Aldington, 'a new cadence is a new idea.' But this notion is far older than the Imagists.

'Any musical innovation is full of danger to the whole state, and ought to be prohibited. When modes of music change, the fundamental laws of the state always change with them. This spirit of license, finding a home, imperceptibly penetrates into manners and customs. It invades contracts between man and man, and from contracts goes on to laws and constitutions, in utter recklessness, ending at last by an overthrow of all rights, private as well as public.'

So wrote Plato, in the Fourth Book of his *Republic*.

IV

The Poetry of T. S. Eliot

THERE is a legend that when Picasso was asked who
were the younger painters, he replied, 'I am.' In the
same way, if we ask who are the younger poets, the
answer must be: Mr. Eliot. I am not going to discuss
the value of Mr. Eliot's poetry; I am concerned only
with his significance for the poetry of our time, and
with his poetical processes. The greatest tribute a
literary historian can pay to a living poet is to treat
him as if he were dead, pulling no punches, and not
afraid of the poet answering back and contradicting
him. It is, of course, very dangerous to explain a poet's
poetry to his face. I remember, many years ago, after
hearing Mr. I. A. Richards' strange analysis of *A
Cooking Egg*, telling the author about it, and particularly
of the view that 'the red-eyed scavengers' creeping
from Kentish Town and Golders Green were Mr.
Eliot's favourite rats, this time with red eyes, and Mr.
Eliot assured me, with his hand on his heart, that he
had never looked a rat in the eyes.

I have, in previous sections, dealt with the Symbolist
strain in modern poetry, and with the Imagist movement which originated with T. E. Hulme and was set
in order by Ezra Pound. The fighting and the fusing
of these two strains, the therapeutic tightness and
hardness of the Imagists, and the sometimes clotted,
three-piled imagery of the Symbolists, is at the back

of all modern verse. But this, of course, over-simplifies the picture. Movements can be dealt with in wide sweeps, but an individual poet must be scrutinised with minute attention. Mr. Eliot is so much the parent of to-day's poetry, and the midwife of to-day's method, that the historian of present-day poetry has the paramount duty of saying, or trying to say, what exactly happened to him in the years leading to the publication of the *Prufrock* volume, and what happened between *Prufrock* and *The Waste Land.*

In 1919 Mr. Eliot said of Shakespeare: 'We need a great many facts in his biography; and we should like to know whether, and when, and after or at the same time as what personal experience, he read Montaigne's *Apologie de Raimond Sebond.*' We have to ask a similar question of Mr. Eliot. Although we may be treating him, for our purposes, as a corpse, he is very much alive, so why must we go on guessing? We can't ask Shakespeare, he's dead. Why can't we ask Mr. Eliot plainly: 'When did you first meet Mr. Ezra Pound? What did you say to each other? What books did he make you read? What made you write *Morning at the Window?*' In other words, 'What did you and Ben Jonson talk about at the Mermaid Tavern?' Even if we did ask, I am not sure that we should get an answer.

> Others abide our question. Thou art free.
> We ask and ask: Thou smilest and art still.

Let us try to piece the story together, and start from the beginning. Mr. Eliot was born in September 1888. He went to Harvard in the autumn of 1906. In 1910 and 1911 he was in Paris, studying philosophy and French literature. He was back in America in 1911, spending three years studying logic, metaphysics, psychology and Sanskrit. He was in Germany before the outbreak of war in 1914. The following winter he was at Oxford reading Greek philosophy, and in 1917 he published his first volume, *Prufrock and other Observations*. 1917 is a long time ago, yet it must often have been thought queer that in 1917 a man of twenty-nine should be writing in so adolescent and *fin de siècle* a manner. But *The Love Song of J. Alfred Prufrock* does not date from 1917. It only began to reach a wider public in that year. It had reached its select public in 1915. But—the poem was written as far back as 1911. What seemed raving lunacy in 1915 was still very strange in 1917, and is still, in 1951, very strange to hundreds of thousands of sincere and puzzled readers. Written in 1911 it was by way of being a miracle.

The shock of *Prufrock*[*] came in the startling opening image:

> Let us go then, you and I,
> When the evening is spread out against the sky
> Like a patient etherized upon a table;

It lay in the strange animal imagery of the fog:

> The yellow fog that rubs its back upon the window-
> panes,
> The yellow smoke that rubs its muzzle on the
> window-panes,
> Licked its tongue into the corners of the evening, . . .
>
> Slipped by the terrace, made a sudden leap,
> And seeing that it was a soft October night,
> Curled once about the house, and fell asleep.

---

* From *Collected Poems 1909–1935* by T. S. Eliot, copyright 1936, by Harcourt, Brace and Company, Inc.

It lay in the irony, the lunatic incoherencies and disconnectedness, the unrelated asides, the unpoetic language, the colloquialisms intermingled with romantic and Shakespearean lines, the sharp juxtapositions, the pertinent irrelevances:

> I should have been a pair of ragged claws
> Scuttling across the floors of silent seas.

in the citations and allusions, the startling effects:

> I have measured out my life with coffee spoons;

> And I have seen the eternal Footman hold my coat, and snicker.

There was the individual accent and cadence:

> Shall I part my hair behind? Do I dare to eat a peach?
> I shall wear white flannel trousers, and walk upon the beach.

There was the super-modernity of the sum-total, the unity of atmosphere built up of fragments, the exploration of what we now realise to be the logic of the unconscious, and the picture of what we now recognise as an inferiority complex. It seems a frightening catalogue, and I make this analysis in order to separate out a few of the elements which contemporaries lumped together with a shudder of uncomprehending rejection.

Was this parthenogenesis, or had it parents? It had. What was new in England and America was already old elsewhere, in France. 'The French poets,' wrote Mr. Eliot, 'have made discoveries in verse of which we cannot afford to be ignorant.' These poets were Baudelaire, Verlaine, Laforgue and Corbière. The common quality we recognise in *Prufrock*, in *Rhapsody on a Windy Night*, *Conversation Galante* and *Portrait of a Lady* is mainly the quality, the note, the accent, the mood of Jules Laforgue. *Prufrock* was written in 1911 in Paris and Munich, *Rhapsody on a Windy Night* was written in Paris the same year, *Portrait of a Lady* in 1910, and *Conversation Galante* as early as 1909. Startling and disturbing dates, upsetting all our ideas. This poetic force appears, then, not as a mushroom growth in 1917, but in steady evolution from as far back as 1909. These important dates are given by Mr. John Hayward, on Mr. Eliot's own authority, in the French translation of the poems by Pierre Leyris, and Mr. Hayward has written some very valuable additional notes to *The Waste Land* for this same edition. The mere affixing of these bibliographical data is exciting enough in itself, but there is a further batch of evidence from which we can reconstruct the earliest developments of Mr. Eliot's poetry. While at Harvard he contributed a number of poems to a periodical, *The Harvard Advocate*. These were reprinted in that journal in December 1938, and among others there is the earliest poem Mr. Eliot is known to have written, a song written and printed in a school magazine early in 1905, when he was only sixteen and a half. Here it is:

If space and time, as sages say
　　Are things that cannot be,
The fly that lives a single day
　　Has lived as long as we.
But let us live while yet we may,
　　While love and life are free,
For time is time, and runs away,
　　Though sages disagree.

The flowers I sent thee when the dew
  Was trembling on the vine
Were withered ere the wild bee flew
  To suck the eglantine.
But let us haste to pluck anew
  Nor mourn to see them pine,
And though the flowers of life be few
  Yet let them be divine.

This is pastiche, of course, of Ben Jonson and Waller and the like, but what brilliant pastiche, the technical gift is already mature, the music is retained, the phrases echoed, there is a simple and naïve mosaic. Other poems show the influence of Rossetti and Swinburne, and possibly through Swinburne a touch of Baudelaire. But there are three poems, all with French titles, which show his progress. *Nocturne* is the first of the new style. *Humoresque* is plainly labelled 'After J. Laforgue', and its first line,

One of my marionettes is dead,

is a free rendering of Laforgue's 'Un de mes pierrots est mort'. But the most interesting is *Spleen*:

Sunday: this satisfied procession
Of definite Sunday faces;
Bonnets, silk hats, and conscious graces
In repetition that displaces
Your mental self-possession
By this unwarranted digression.

Evening, lights, and tea!
Children and cats in the alley;
Dejection unable to rally
Against this dull conspiracy.

4

And Life, a little bald and gray,
Languid, fastidious, and bland,
Waits, hat and gloves in hand,
Punctilious of tie and suit
(Somewhat impatient of delay)
On the doorstep of the Absolute.

This was written a good year before *Prufrock*, and seems a trial-piece for it. It is a little anthology almost, of Laforgue, and Baudelaire and Verlaine. 'Spleen', in its French sense of melancholy and sadness, is a common theme among the French poets. Laforgue has a dozen poems on the horrors of Sunday. The same stage properties are used, and they recur in *Prufrock*—the bald head, the hat and gloves, the tie and suit. The formal polysyllables are borrowed, and from Verlaine's *Croquis Parisien* Mr. Eliot borrows the cat in the alley, which he uses again in the *Rhapsody on a Windy Night*, written the next year in Paris itself, where the dead geranium comes from Corbière, and the French quotation 'La lune ne garde aucune rancune' is nearly from Laforgue.

One quality which emerges in these poems, collected and uncollected, the poems of 1911 and before, is the sense of place, which comes from Baudelaire, who, wrote Mr. Eliot, 'gave new possibilities to poetry in a new stock of imagery of contemporary life, but it is not merely in the use of imagery of common life, not merely in the use of imagery of the sordid life of a great metropolis, but in the elevation of such imagery to the *first intensity*, presenting it as it is, and yet making it represent something much more than itself, that Baudelaire has created a mode of release and expression for other men'. Some poets, such as Baudelaire, he says, 'turn directly to the littered streets, the squinting slums, the grime and smoke and the viscid human life within the streets, and find there the centre of intensity'. This mood, passing through Verlaine's *Croquis Parisien*, is what gives us the cats in lamp-lit alleys, the one-night cheap hotels, the smells of steaks in passage-ways.

The war has begun, Mr. Eliot has left Germany, and in the autumn of 1914 is in England. Then comes the great event—the meeting with Ezra Pound. In September 1914 Pound writes of him to an American friend: 'I think he has some sense, though he has not sent me any verse.' On September 30, 1914, he writes: 'I was jolly well right about Eliot. He has sent in the best poem I have yet had or seen from an American. PRAY GOD IT BE NOT A SINGLE AND UNIQUE SUCCESS. . . . He has actually trained himself *and* modernized himself *on his own*.' He sent *Prufrock* to be printed in the Chicago magazine *Poetry* in June 1915, and in November 1915 included it in his *Catholic Anthology* together with *Portrait of a Lady* and the newly written *Boston Evening Transcript* and *Miss Helen Slingsby*. Pound at this time was the leader, the bear-leader almost, of the Imagist movement. Its reputation had spread. Mr. Eliot was certainly aware of it. Pound had printed T. E. Hulme's poems at the end of his own *Ripostes*, and I hope I am not wrong in supposing that *Morning at the Window*, written at Oxford in 1915, owes something to the Imagist movement.

The important year seems to have been 1917. In that year Mr. Eliot was appointed literary editor of *The Egoist*. Ezra Pound poured out his erudition and

technical experience, and received in return the imprint
of a poetical personality. Many things bound them
together—the French poets of the Laforgue style,
Dante, the Metaphysical Poets, and the later Elizabethans. Mr. Eliot did not need Mr. Pound to tell
him about Laforgue. Laforgue was a newcomer in
Pound's world. Pound's real love was Provençal
poetry—the Troubadours. Mr. Eliot did not need to
be told of the late Elizabethans or of the Metaphysicals.
In *Whispers of Immortality,** written in 1917, the year of
the fateful discussions, Mr. Eliot wrote of them both.

> Webster was much possessed by death
> And saw the skull beneath the skin;
> And breastless creatures under ground
> Leaned backward with a lipless grin.
>
> Daffodil bulbs instead of balls
> Stared from the sockets of the eyes!
> He knew that thought clings round dead limbs
> Tightening its lusts and luxuries.
>
> Donne, I suppose, was such another
> Who found no substitute for sense;
> To seize and clutch and penetrate,
> Expert beyond experience.
>
> He knew the anguish of the marrow,
> The ague of the skeleton;
> No contact possible to flesh
> Allayed the fever of the bone.

But in that same poem is a new note and a new verse.
The free verse is abandoned, and early that same year
sees Mr. Eliot's essay, still fascinating, called *Reflections*

* From *Collected Poems 1909–1935* by T. S. Eliot, copyright 1936, by
Harcourt, Brace and Company, Inc.

on Vers Libre, in which he renounces it. The verse of
*Whispers of Immortality** is a new verse, a tight verse, not
a free verse, a close four-lined stanza using careful
rhyme, which comes from Théophile Gautier's *Emaux
et Camées,* to which Ezra Pound had redirected his
attention. From Gautier, just as he had done with
Laforgue, he borrows tunes, and plays variants on them.

> Grishkin is nice: her Russian eye
> Is underlined for emphasis;
> Uncorseted, her friendly bust
> Gives promise of pneumatic bliss.

This is Gautier's *Carmen est maigre,* but with a difference.
It is always with a difference. He is perfecting a
twofold technique, of allusion to and incorporation of
other men's verses, and the Metaphysical technique of
dealing in body and soul together, in abstract and
concrete, in intellect and emotion. Three essential
strains come together, Webster, Donne and Gautier,
and the result is the characteristic tone of Mr. Eliot's
second phase, which concludes the poem:

> And even the Abstract Entities
> Circumambulate her charm;
> But our lot crawls between dry ribs
> To keep our metaphysics warm.

In *Mr. Eliot's Sunday Morning Service** his personal voice
becomes more confident and recognisable:

> Polyphiloprogenitive
> The sapient sutlers of the Lord
> Drift across the window-panes.
> In the beginning was the Word.

* From *Collected Poems 1909–1935* by T. S. Eliot, copyright 1936, by
Harcourt, Brace and Company, Inc.

The same tunes persist in *Sweeney among the Nightingales,*
the measured march of solemn writing about an
apparently trivial subject-matter, poker-faced poetry:

> The person in the Spanish cape
> Tries to sit on Sweeney's knees
>
> Slips and pulls the table cloth
> Overturns a coffee-cup,
> Reorganised upon the floor
> She yawns and draws a stocking up;

We are moving already toward *The Waste Land.*

> When lovely woman stoops to folly and
> Paces about her room again, alone,
> She smoothes her hair with automatic hand,
> And puts a record on the gramophone.

Here things are happening on the surface and things
are happening below the surface, the double-take as it
were, the sober face and the illumination that follows,
the spirit of dry and controlled and directed parody.
There is precedent for it in Laforgue's bitter parody
of *Au clair de la lune.*

The chief device which Mr. Eliot has taught modern
poets, and which has become the standard device of
modern poetry, is that method of incorporating a line
from some other poet, or some other language, deftly
converted, deftly conveyed, its license-plates so altered
that its own proprietor would hardly recognise it. It is
a device used not for mere decoration, or even wit, but
to produce reverberations of meaning, and above all of
feeling. It is a process which reaches its climax in the
climactic conclusion of *The Waste Land,* a passage

---

* From *Collected Poems 1909–1935* by T. S. Eliot, copyright 1936, by
Harcourt, Brace and Company, Inc.

comparable to the scintillations at the end of D. W. Griffith's film *Intolerance*, where the climaxes of the several stories are interwoven into a beatitude of swift cutting, unparalleled emotionally outside the Russian masters who followed him.

What is the ancestry of the end of *The Waste Land*? Let us make a little detour, let us go on a little pilgrimage. In Miss Edith Sitwell's fine poem *Still falls the Rain*,[*] written in the air-raids of 1940, there is a remarkable passage:

> Still falls the Rain—
> Then—O Ile leape up to my God: who pulles me
> doune—
> See, see where Christ's blood streames in the
> firmament:
> It flows from the Brow we nailed upon the tree
> Deep to the dying, to the thirsting heart
> That holds the fires of the world,—dark-smirched
> with pain
> As Cæsar's laurel crown.

This sudden flash, 'Ile leape up to my God', is a direct quotation from Marlowe's *Faustus*, used to concentrate and to canalise an emotion, not because the author has none of her own, but because the tension is so high that only a great emotion could fit in, and she knows that here Marlowe will not only not let her down, but will lift her up. The passage is superb in itself, its music is self-explanatory for those who know no more. But let us jump back three hundred and fifty years, to Marlowe's play itself, the last scene when Faustus, having sold his soul to the devil, tries to put off the imminent hour of delivery, the famous soliloquy:

* Copyright 1949, by Edith Sitwell

Stand still, you ever-moving spheres of heaven,
That time may cease, and midnight never come;
Fair Nature's eye, rise, rise again, and make
Perpetual day; or let this hour be but
A year, a month, a week, a natural day,
That Faustus may repent and save his soul!
O lente, lente currite, noctis equi!
The stars move still, time runs, the clock will
strike,
The devil will come, and Faustus must be damn'd.
O, I'll leap up to my God!—Who pulls me down?—
See, see, where Christ's blood streams in the
firmament!
One drop would save my soul, half a drop: ah,
my Christ!
Rend not my heart for naming of my Christ!
Yet will I call on him! O, spare me, Lucifer!—

Now we see what the poet is calling upon to support
her poem, one agony is reinforced by another agony.
But, what do we find? Marlowe, writing for an
audience of notorious groundlings, inserts a line of
Latin verse: *O lente, lente currite, noctis equi!* What is
the point of this line—the sense is complete without it—
yet it must be there for a purpose? Mr. Eliot says a
shrewd and fundamental thing about Shakespeare.
'In a play of Shakespeare you get several levels of
significance. For the simplest auditors there is the
plot, for the more thoughtful the characters and
conflict of characters, for the more literary the words
and phrasing, for the more musically sensitive the
rhythm, and for auditors of greater sensitiveness and
understanding a meaning which reveals itself gradually.
At none of these levels is the auditor bothered by the

presence of that which he does not understand, or by the presence of that in which he is not interested.' The most remarkable thing about the Elizabethan audience is the colossal amount of poetry it would stand on its way to blood and thunder. Mr. Eliot puts it much better in a letter to Ezra Pound on the principles of dramatic writing. 'If the audience gets its strip-tease it will swallow the poetry.' What, then, is the point of inserting this Latin verse—'run slowly, slowly, you horses of the night'? It comes from Ovid's poem to the dawn, which Marlowe himself translated. It is the lover begging the night to linger so that dawn may not come to tear his love from his arms. The groundling gets his strip-tease, but the lover of poetry gets his bonus. In this speech, too, there are echoes from the Book of Revelation, and the grand climax 'I'll burn my books' calls on the nineteenth chapter of the Acts of the Apostles. Shakespeare learnt from Marlowe, and we all learn from Shakespeare.

Now let us continue our circular tour, back to Mr. Eliot. Marlowe uses this method, Shakespeare uses it, Dante uses it, and it is from Dante that Mr. Eliot takes it most directly. Of all Mr. Eliot's critical writings two works stand out: his superb study of Dante, and his subtle and revealing essay *The Music of Poetry*. Between them they hold and they reveal Mr. Eliot's innermost secrets as a poet, his standards, his methods, and his beliefs *as a poet*. Of the many things he owes to Ezra Pound the chief is his debt for the path to the understanding of Dante. They shared an awed admiration for one passage in the *Purgatorio* where Dante's poetical master Guido Guinicelli points to Arnaut Daniel the Provençal poet as a better craftsman of the mother-tongue, Daniel, the master of the obscure style in poetry. *The Waste Land* is dedicated to Ezra Pound in those very words—*il miglior fabbro*—the better craftsman. But what is more exciting, Dante makes Arnaut Daniel speak, not in Italian, but in Provençal—in a speech playing on the opening of one of Daniel's own poems. Here is Dante using Mr. Eliot's own method, and Mr. Eliot repays him by using this passage time and time again: 'Ara vos prec.' 'Je vous prie.' ' "Now I pray you, by that goodness which guideth you to the summit of the stairway, be mindful in due time of my pain." Then he hid himself in the fire which refines them.' *Ara vos prec* is the title of the volume printed at the Ovid Press by Mr. John Rodker in 1920. 'Al som de l'escalina'—'to the summit of the stairway'—is the original title of the third section of *Ash Wednesday*. The words 'sovegna vos' (be mindful) occur in *Ash Wednesday*, and the Italian line which concludes the passage is part of the mosaic-conclusion to *The Waste Land*—'the scrap-heap of quotation' as Mr. E. M. Forster called it. 'These fragments I have shored against my ruins.' Never was so little of one poet's work used so much by another poet. What is said in the conclusion to *The Waste Land* is said not in the lines quoted, but in the setting from which they are taken. The poet keeps his secret for those who have earned the right to receive it.

One last word, on the music of Mr. Eliot's poetry. A poet convinces, and from the most primitive times has convinced, not by the words he says but by the tune to which he says them, or, as Mr. Eliot has said, 'poetry can communicate before it is understood'. This ugly, harsh, prose-writing poet, as he has variously been called, is a master of music—not the obvious *Blessed Damozel* style of *La Figlia che Piange*, but the subtle counterpointed style of his later work. Let a poet call his volume *Four Quartets* and there creeps into the wise and collective noddle of the public a faint suspicion that it may, possibly, have something to do with music, and the public shakes its noddle and says, 'why yes—of course—sonata form' and so forth. Mr. Eliot has found a name for that special approach to language which leads to this music. He calls it 'the auditory imagination'. 'What I call the "auditory imagination",' he says, 'is the feeling for syllable and rhythm, penetrating far below the conscious levels of thought and feeling, invigorating every word; sinking to the most primitive and forgotten, returning to the origin and bringing something back, seeking the beginning and the end.' That is why the poet must link himself with tradition and even with the tradition that existed before tradition began. The poet, advised Ezra Pound, should 'fill his mind with the finest cadences he can discover, . . . Saxon charms, Hebridean Folk Songs, the verse of Dante and the lyrics of Shakespeare, if he can dissociate the vocabulary from the cadence.' Mr. Eliot followed that advice. Here is a typical piece of Eliot music:

> Since drought has come upon the land,
> And that we do not expect rarity,
> A little of the substance of the summer,
>   Would we desire with the bread.

I don't know *where* it occurs in his poetry, I don't even know *whether* it occurs in his poetry, but it sounds like a chorus in *Murder in the Cathedral*. I found it where Mr. Eliot must have found it, in a volume of Gaelic hymns and incantations.

I have spoken only of the earlier poems, of the interstitial melody and the simple counterpoint. In the *Four Quartets* we advance to symphonic music, music of sound and sense and correspondences, retracings and echoes, and bells rung and tolled in the distance. Picture and mood and opinion, thought and belief and despair, and possibly even hope, are interwoven in a musical tapestry. The terror seems to be softening, the abyss has been looked into, the spider no longer terrifies, and with his beloved Dante the poet may yet pass from the Inferno to the Paradiso.

V

Poetry and Science

THERE is a widespread belief that modern poetry is
marked by a special awareness of modern science, that
scientific imagery pervades the more alert and advanced
poetry of to-day, and that poets faced by the pressure
and complexity of the new scientific pattern of life are
changing their very modes of feeling and expression.
How far is this true? We cannot answer this question
without first asking another question. Is it true that
at *any* time the incursions of science have so changed
the fundamental beliefs of man in relation to his
circumambient universe, as to force him to change
the shape and the tune of the song with which he
celebrates the glories of that universe? I say the
fundamental beliefs, because there is more than a
suspicion that it is only the surface beliefs, the surface
patterns which alter, the surface idiom. Is mankind
really interested in the fundamental changes, and does
mankind, through its poet-spokesmen, record these
changes?

Poetry must communicate, if necessary communicate
before it is understood. You can communicate with
some of the people all the time, you can communicate
with all of the people some of the time, but it is vain
to hope to communicate with all of the people all of
the time. If the poetry is genuine, there is communication with somebody—for the poet is a prophet

only in so far as he has an audience in his own time. To wait for the future with which he is already abreast is to deliver his message too late. The poet should point out what is happening *while* it is happening, he is not there to deliver funeral orations. This, if it is true, places a terrible burden of responsibility on the poet. His antennæ must be moving, his feelers waving with a feverish intensity.

What is modern science for the modern man? What is the *un*scientific man aware of? What is the common reference-ground the poet can rely on? What is the basic language he must use for communication? What is the common universe of discourse? What, in short, are the clichés and common currency of science for the modern unscientific man? Is it Radar, or is it the atomic bomb? Does it reside in vast shocks or in comforting curiosities? Atomic bombs are too spectacular for any serious deeper emotions to be roused. There is no *process* that the poetic mind can wrap itself around. The simple man can realise only the secondary implications, the mushroom cloud of smoke, the seared flesh and the cold fear of sterility, and the theologian is confronted with yet another neurosis of guilt. There must always be an emotional response, not a mere intellectual recognition, but the emotional response must be in essence direct and not secondary. For science to reach mankind vague associations are of no value. Einstein means nothing, relativity means nothing, a 'finite universe' or 'curvature of space' are just pretty phrases. I do not believe that Einstein has given one real image to poetry, not even a decorative or a witty image.

But Freud is different, Freud and the science of the mind. There must be a warm association, fear-making or hope-making, or something even more minutely specific, like Pavlov's conditioned reflex. We can believe that; the swan answers the food-bell, the dog's mouth waters.

It is such specific convictions that science can give to the poet, something to cling to on the dizzy journey. If I were a poet I should have been awakened by those scientific films, direct-action films, we used to show at the old Film Society. To see the circulation of the blood, the torrents of blood racing over the surface of the screen, was to believe. To watch a shapeless splinter of bone growing inexorably into a shapely and complete thigh-bone of a chicken, is to believe in the purposive inevitability of giant nature. These are personal associations, of course, lucky dips which occur only rarely, and unless one is a poet, unusable and unprofitable. The poet is one of those lucky people whose lottery tickets are all prize-winners.

I am concerned, not with the values of science, ultimate or immediate, but only with what concerns mankind and his interpreter the poet.

The last big pervasive shock was Darwin, and all the vague derivatives associated with his name. In our own time the most startling, getting right under the skin, was Freud with his contribution to the science of the mind. It dawns on us that the only sciences or scientific advances which widely affect mankind, outside the specialist or the utilitarian sphere, are those which administer blows to man's self-esteem, affect his conceit of himself, or change his estimate of his place in the universe. With Darwin there was the grave suspicion in the popular mind that the family tree was arboreal rather than heraldic, and with Freud there was the fear that the unknown, the hidden, the obscene, would be made public. 'Surely we are not as bad as all that' was the guilty cry.

The great landmarks in this direction, going back in time, are Newton, Galileo, Kepler and Copernicus, and between them they shook man out of his complacency, jolted him from his smug position at the centre of the universe and made him shift for himself. Before then, great poets, like Dante and Chaucer, were permeated with science, but it was a science of belief, not of doubt.

It is with John Donne that poetry first feels the shock of science, and curiously enough, at the highest pitch at which this conjunction is possible. In 1610 he wrote the famous lines:

> And new Philosophy calls all in doubt,
> The Element of fire is quite put out;
> The Sun is lost, and th'earth, and no mans wit
> Can well direct him where to looke for it.

Behind these lines and their sequel lies one of those stories which justify literary history. Copernicus died in 1543, but his startling theory, that the sun and not the earth was the centre of our universe, made little headway, even though Giordano Bruno told Sir Philip Sidney and the other English poets about it forty years later. It made no difference to practical life which moved, earth or sun. The first general shock to this complacency came when Tycho Brahe discovered a

new star in Cassiopeia in 1572—but Brahe was no
Copernicus, and people while accepting the fact of
his discovery dared not accept its implications.
Obstinacy was useless, however, when Kepler discovered *his* new star in 1604 and when Galileo in 1610
announced his four new planets in Jupiter. Facts
just had to be faced. But what was all the excitement
about? Why all this fuss about a star or a planet
more or less? It was not just a matter of one planet
more or less, it was a question of the foundations of
all belief. As Donne wrote to the Countess of Bedford:

> We have added to the world Virginia, and sent
> Two new starres lately to the firmament.

For nearly two thousand years, ever since Aristotle, the
universe had been fixed and unchangeable, the heavenly
bodies were numbered and this number could in no
circumstances be altered, and now these new mad-
men were cooking the accounts. The earlier thinkers
had believed without proof. Some of the later ones
had proof without belief. Giordano Bruno believed
in infinite space and a plurality of worlds, but could
see nothing. Kepler saw new stars but did not accept
the implications. Galileo, through his telescope, saw
new worlds and believed in what they implied.

Where does John Donne come into this story? On
the very day of the publication of Galileo's *Siderius
Nuncius*, 'The Messenger of the Stars', the 13th of
March 1610, Donne's friend, Sir Henry Wotton, our
Ambassador in Venice, sent home a copy for the
King with a promise to send one of the new telescopes.
Whether he also sent a copy to Donne we have no

5

means of knowing, but what we do know is that in 1610 Donne wrote a prose satire, published next year, *Ignatius his Conclave*, playing with the ideas of Copernicus, and Kepler and Galileo, and very fully aware of their position in the overthrow of the old scientific order. Wotton had not only summarised Galileo's startling findings, but had shrewdly put his finger on a point to which Donne returns time and time again. 'Galileo,' he said, 'has first overthrown all former astronomy, and next all *astrology*,' and it was the astrology that mattered.

Astrology was the science which studied the specific influence of the stars on human destiny, and for this science a fixed universe was essential. Add but one star and 'chaos is come again'. Galileo added millions of new stars. Dante and Chaucer and Shakespeare are poets of the fixed universe. Donne and Milton are unstable as water, fluctuating between the Ptolemaic and the Copernican heavens. Astrology died hard. It still lives in the Sunday newspapers, and during the last war both Hitler and our counter-intelligence took it very seriously indeed. The new science had now passed beyond the scientists to the people. Although Copernicanism had been vaguely in the air, it was Kepler and, above all, Galileo who forced them into belief. It was the telescope, something they could handle, something through which they could see for themselves, that fired the imagination.

And what did Galileo claim to have seen? Four new planets, the detailed miracle of the Milky Way, with its myriads of stars never seen before, and, much nearer home, the moon! 'It is a most beautiful and delightful sight,' he said, 'to behold the body of the Moon, just like the face of the Earth itself, is everywhere full of vast protuberances, deep chasms and sinuosities.' The moon! I have suggested that the history of poetry seems to be the poet's search after new images for the moon. But I anticipate.

Donne had written in prose in 1610, and had also written in verse, for the first time assimilating the new science into his all-devouring mechanism of poetry. The passage whose beginning I have already quoted, from *The Anatomy of the World*, printed in 1611, is the classic passage of unsurpassed and often unsuspected richness:

> And new Philosophy calls all in doubt,
> The Element of fire is quite put out;
> The Sun is lost, and th'earth, and no mans wit
> Can well direct him where to looke for it.
> And freely men confesse that this world's spent,
> When in the Planets, and the Firmament
> They seeke so many new; then see that this
> Is crumbled out againe to his Atomies.
> 'Tis all in peeces, all cohaerence gone;
> All just supply, and all Relation:
> Prince, Subject, Father, Sonne, are things forgot,
> For every man alone thinkes he hath got
> To be a Phœnix, and that then can bee
> None of that kinde, of which he is, but hee.

This 'New Philosophy' is what we should call the New Science. Hamlet tells Horatio there are more things in heaven and earth than *science* dreams of, and there are still Chairs of Natural Philosophy in the Universities. 'The Element of fire is quite put out.' Paracelsus had undermined another article of faith.

The four elements were air, earth, fire and water, and he had denied that fire was an element. The elements are still important for poetry. The most beautiful section of Mr. Eliot's *Four Quartets* relies on this age-old material for its force.

This is the death of air.

*   *   *

This is the death of earth.

*   *   *

This is the death of water and fire.*]

'The sun is lost and th'earth,' 'these mad carmen who drive the earth about' have upset all normal relationship. The old world is worn out, we seek new planets in the Firmament. ''Tis all in peeces, all cohaerence gone': the fixed order of the universe has been shaken up, the fixed hierarchy of society is broken, 'Prince, Subject, Father, Sonne, are things forgot', individual man is thrown on his own resources. And how does the poem continue?

This is the worlds condition now, and now
She that should all parts to reunion bow,
She that had all Magnetique force alone,
To draw, and fasten sundred parts in one;

*   *   *

Shee, shee is dead; shee's dead:

I have already spoken of the value of poetry to historians, its value in helping them to gauge the permeation among the people, for instance, of the idea of Magna Carta. Now we can see the value of

* From "Little Gidding" in *Four Quartets,* copyright 1943, by T. S. Eliot. Reprinted by permission of Harcourt, Brace and Company, Inc.

poetry to the historian of science. This to us casual phrase 'Magnetique force' is startling, for it is a proof that Gilbert's doctrine of magnetism had spread, at least to John Donne, and this use of the word 'magnetic' is nearly a quarter of a century earlier than the earliest illustration in the Oxford Dictionary. This is modern scientific poetry with a vengeance. Our modern poets of 'this scientific age' certainly seem justified in taking John Donne for their patron saint. There are dozens of scientific allusions in Donne, but not all of them are contemporary, many are still mediæval, and few are of the complexity or intensity of the passage whose surface I have only scratched. But there is one passage which has never been fully expounded, I think, and which to me is perhaps Donne's loveliest, in intrinsic achievement. A poet is always moonstruck, and Donne, in his famous *Valediction: Of Weeping* reaches a climax in the last stanza.

> O more than Moone,
> Draw not up seas to drown me in thy spheare,
> Weepe me not dead, in thine armes, but forbeare
> To teach the sea, what it may doe too soone;
>   Let not the winde
>   Example finde,
> To doe me more harme, than it purposeth;
> Since thou and I sigh one anothers breath,
> Who e'r sighes most, is cruellest, and hastes the
>   others death.

What is there to expound? This is perfectly clear: the pull of the moon and the mounting tides. But wait. When was this written? Even if it is no earlier than the day of Donne's death in 1631, Newton did not announce this doctrine till at least fifty years later. Is the poet ahead of the scientist, divinely guessing, or is there some other explanation? There is. The doctrine, sufficient, at any rate, for the poet's needs, is in Kepler. We have forgotten it in Newton's greater glory, but there Donne must have found it, and that perhaps throws a new light on the date of the poem.

The moon! The next poet who goes moon-watching is Milton, and he illustrates the second way in which poetry and science can meet: a lower intensity than Donne's way, but still very high tension, not the incorporated, not the creatively assimilative method, but the strongly emotional descriptive or allusive method. In the First Book of *Paradise Lost* is the famous passage, 'Satan all armed with his attendant legions':

> He scarce had ceased when the superior Fiend
> Was moving toward the shore; his ponderous shield,
> Ethereal temper, massy, large and round,
> Behind him cast. The broad circumference
> Hung on his shoulders like the moon, whose orb
> Through optic glass the Tuscan artist views
> At evening from the top of Fesole,
> Or in Valdarno, to descry new lands,
> Rivers, or mountains, in her spotty globe.

The moon! The 'Tuscan artist' is Galileo, the 'optic glass' is the telescope. 'From the top of Fesole,' above Florence, 'to descry new lands, rivers or mountains, in her spotty globe'. The 'spotty globe' is the new cliché for the moon, soon to join the zombied ranks of poetic diction, but this I think is its first use, the coin is bright and fresh-minted, and this is the first appearance of Galileo and his telescope in poetry of any magnitude.   But the passage is not ended.

>   on the beach
> Of that inflamed sea he stood, and called
> His legions, Angel forms, who lay entranced,
> Thick as autumnal leaves that strow the brooks
> In Vallambrosa, where the Etrurian shades
> High over-arched embower.

Why is this passage so powerful and so memorable? There is nothing of the metaphysical pattern of complexity about it, and it is, in both its parts, composed of simple simile.   The point is that Milton, as a blind persecuted revolutionary, is remembering another blind persecuted revolutionary, who through his optic glass had seen more than other mortals. The poet recalled the intensity of his own vision, when he still had vision, not of the moon in the heavens, but the leaves at his feet, the autumnal leaves. This descent, from the scientific heavens to the concrete earth, is as effective as Donne's very different swoop from Heaven to earth in his Holy Sonnet:

> Thy Grace may wing me to prevent his art,
> And thou like Adamant draw mine iron heart.

Or, in secular mood, the same concrete force in *The Will:*

> And all your graces no more use shall have
> Than a Sun dyall in a grave.

One gift of the new science to poetry was a sense of limitless space, to last until Einstein closed these vast immensities into a finite universe in our own day.

Donne threads the planets on a string of cosmic speed, and Milton's Satan moves in an infinity of space.

The lowest form of contact between poetry and science is the purely descriptive, and the lowest period is the eighteenth century, the century which had the noblest opportunity. It had Newton. Yet of the hundreds of specimens Miss Marjorie Nicolson gives in her fascinating book *Newton Demands the Muse*, not one shows the poet realising the possibilities of science for the serious writing of poetry. Alexander Pope, in his revision of *The Rape of the Lock*, uses it only for wit and fantasy.

Newton had to wait for his turn. In 1704 he wrote: 'In a very dark Chamber, at a round hole, about one third part of an Inch broad, made in the Shut of a Window, I placed a Glass Prism, whereby the Beam of the Sun's Light, which came in at that Hole, might be refracted upwards toward the opposite Wall of the Chamber, and there form a coloured Image of the Sun.' And long after, in 1821, Shelley wrote in his *Adonais*:

> Life, like a dome of many-coloured glass,
> Stains the white radiance of Eternity,
> Until Death tramples it to fragments.

It is not always easy to detect the science in Shelley, so digested is it, so alembicated. Without a clue, what would we make of this in his early poem *Queen Mab*?

> The sun's unclouded orb
> Rolled through the black concave.

Shelley's own footnote tells us the background of these two lines. 'Beyond our atmosphere the sun would appear a rayless orb of fire in the midst of a black concave. The equal diffusion of its light on earth is owing to the refraction of the rays by the atmosphere, and their reflection from other bodies. Light consists either of vibrations propagated through a subtle medium, or of numerous minute particles repelled in all directions from the luminous body' . . . 'in one year light travels 5,422,400,000,000 miles, which is a distance 5,707,600 times greater than that of the sun from the earth.' I find this just as fascinating as Mr. Auden's quotations from Hans Spemann's *Embryonic Development and Induction* in the notes to his *New Year Letter*. 'If a piece of totipotent ectoderm is implanted into the epidermis of another germ, it does not form part of the new surroundings according to the needs of the new place, but gives origin to the most different organs, in accordance with the region of the germ. . . . Still more remarkable are the results of hetero-plastic and xenoplastic induction.' And I am pre-pared to accept Professor Whitehead's verdict that 'What the hills were to the youth of Wordsworth, a chemical laboratory was to Shelley. . . . If Shelley had been born a hundred years later, the twentieth century would have seen a Newton among Chemists'.

Shelley got much of his science from Erasmus Darwin, Charles Darwin's grandfather, a strangely prophetic person whose poetry dominated the end of the eighteenth century. His *Temple of Nature* and his *Botanic Garden* are fascinating works in which, as he said, he tried 'to enlist imagination under the banner of Science, and to lead her votaries from the looser analogies which dress out the imagery of poetry, to the stricter ones which form the ratiocination of philosophy'. His prophecies are more exciting and more specific than Tennyson's 'Airy navies grappling in the central blue':

> Soon shall thy arm, unconquer'd Steam! afar
> Drag the small barge, or drive the rapid car;
> Or on wide-waving wings expanded bear
> The flying chariot through the fields of air.
> Fair crews triumphant, leaning from above,
> Shall wave their fluttering kerchiefs as they move;
> Or warrior-bands alarm the gaping crowd,
> And armies shrink beneath the shadowy cloud.

Tennyson wrote of 'sweet girl graduettes', but he never thought of air-hostesses.

The most famous passage on the relations of poetry and science is Wordsworth's passionate outburst in the 1802 Preface to the *Lyrical Ballads*:

'The Man of Science seeks truth as a remote and unknown benefactor; he cherishes and loves it in his solitude: the Poet, singing a song in which all human beings join with him, rejoices in the presence of truth as our visible friend and hourly companion. Poetry is the breath and finer spirit of all knowledge; it is the impassioned expression which is in the countenance of all Science. . . . If the labours of men of Science should ever create any material revolution, direct or indirect, in our condition, and in the impressions which we habitually receive, the Poet will sleep then no more than at present, but he will be ready to follow the steps of the man of Science, not only in those general indirect effects, but he will be at his side, carrying sensation into the midst of the objects of the Science itself. The remotest discoveries of the Chemist, the Botanist, or Mineralogist, will be as proper objects of the Poet's art as any upon which it can be employed, if the time should ever come when these things shall be familiar to us, and the relations under which they are contemplated by the followers of these respective Sciences shall be manifestly and palpably material to us as enjoying and suffering beings.' What a handsome offer! It sounds like the chairman's address at the annual general meeting of 'Poetry Ltd.' And what did Wordsworth do about it? Precisely nothing. Nothing further was heard about these plans for the expansion of the business. Except for Shelley, and a flash or two from Matthew Arnold and Meredith, there was a lull until modern times.

And what of the moderns? What is left for the moderns to do? Happily, my theme is the Background of Modern Poetry. Had it been the foreground, the moderns would have let me down very badly. I have gone through dozens of volumes and read and re-read hundreds of poems hoping to confirm the belief to which I have referred, that scientific imagery permeates modern poetry, that the poets have been forced by modern science to alter their modes of feeling and expression. Alas! it just isn't true. It is true, of course, that the poets show that they are living in their own age. Mr. Cecil Day Lewis writes:

> Where is the fool would want those days again
> Whose light was globed in pain
> And danced upon a point of wire?

When the charged batteries of desire
Had licence but to pass
Into a narrow room of frosted glass.

and Mr. Louis MacNeice in his *Homage to Clichés*[1] can
write:

These are the moments that are anaplerotic,
  these are the gifts
To be accepted.

The word anaplerotic is not in the Concise Oxford
Dictionary. It means 'medicines that help to fill
ulcers with flesh', a very useful idea, but it is as little
communicated as Shakespeare's technical term
hysterica passio in *King Lear*.

Mr. Stephen Spender can write:

At five a man fell to the ground
And the watch flew off his wrist
Like a moon struck from the earth

But it doesn't carry conviction. He can write about
The Express:

After the first powerful plain manifesto
The black statement of pistons, without more
  fuss
But gliding like a queen, she leaves the station.

and it comes, not from this scientific age, but from this
machine age. Just as most poets have barely caught
up with Baudelaire, so in science and applied science
they are barely beyond the internal combustion
engine, and there must be something more than the
engine, as Mr. Eliot proves in *The Waste Land:* [2]

1. Copyright 1940, by Random House, Inc.
2. Copyright 1936, by Harcourt, Brace and Company, Inc.

At the violet hour, when the eyes and back
Turn upward from the desk, when the human
    engine waits
Like a taxi throbbing waiting,
I Tiresias, though blind, throbbing between two
    lives,
Old man with wrinkled female breasts, can see
At the violet hour, the evening hour that strives
Homeward, and brings the sailor home from
    sea.

The poetry of Mr. Auden and Mr. MacNeice has given rise to a curious syllogism. Their poetry is modern; modern life is scientific; ergo their poetry is scientific. In only one sense is this true, if the dominant science of modernity is sociology. Then a new scientific imagery has been born, not of chemical or physical analysis, but of social implication. In this sense Mr. MacNeice's lines are relevant:

           for fear of germs
Putting on stamps by licking the second finger.
For fear of opinion overtipping in bars.

Or elsewhere:

    'Shall I drink your health before
    The gun-butt raps upon the door?'

These lines contain images of the new science, and 'the brown lace sinking in the empty glass of stout' takes the place of Donne's 'Sun dyall in a grave'. Mr. Auden's hikers and arterial roads and depressed areas and pylons and motor-bikes are also scientific images in this sense. And our conclusion is, not that science, as we usually understand it, dominates the poetry of our time, but that it takes its place for the first time, as an equal alongside the other sciences, as a source of imagery and feeling.

VI

Achievement and Direction

As a literary historian, speaking of the *Background* of
Modern Poetry, I have always spoken with a bias,
that is, I have inevitably taken the historical point of
view. But the literary historian is also required to
have some standards of value, that is to say, to possess
another kind of bias. I confess frankly that my bias
is towards the romantic in poetry, towards poetry
which records and preserves emotion by means of the
forces that lie within words, as a result of their past
experiences, the company they have kept, the ad-
ventures they have had, the emotional and even cultural
accretions they have taken to themselves. I prefer
this way to the classical way, which is a way of using
words as counters, releasing from a kind of automatic
machine a limited, and measured-out portion of
response and reference.

The romantic poet can never know how much poetic
energy he is releasing once he presses his button, or
opens his stopcock, or mixes his metaphors. The
classical poet hopes at least to be in charge of what he
is releasing. From the petrol-pump of classical poetry
you get measured out only the quantity you are paying
for. Romantic poetry gives a perpetual bonus. More-
over, with time, the classical machine gets clogged up,

and delivers progressively less than you have a right to expect.

That is why it is possible to find more 'meaning' in romantic poetry than the poet himself knows. If you ask the poet, 'Did you mean this, or that?' he can legitimately answer, 'Perhaps I did', or even go so far as to answer, 'If you say I meant that, then, of course, I did'. But it should not prevent him from saying firmly, 'But I also meant *this*'—giving his own interpretation.

It is not often that the poet tells us in detail what he means, or meant, at least not often publicly. Between friends, among young poets growing up together, it often happens. It happens most in conversation, it is happening more now in correspondence, it happened in war-time when friends were forcibly separated, and perhaps ultimately these letters will be published. I have heard of some very important exchanges of this kind. One of the most instructive cases comes from America, where so much important poetry is being written. I have tried from time to time to subject the poetic process to analysis, the symbolist method of Mallarmé, the allusive method of Marlowe and T. S. Eliot, the mental process of John Donne, but here is a modern poet telling about his own processes, his modern mechanism. Hart Crane, who killed himself in 1932, wrote *At Melville's Tomb*. Hart Crane has had a profound influence on modern American verse, and where he is known in this country, has gained disciples. It is a difficult poem, but like many modern poems, more difficult to the eye than to the ear. It should be read aloud.

Often beneath the wave, wide from this ledge
The dice of drowned men's bones he saw bequeath
An embassy. Their numbers as he watched,
Beat on the dusty shore and were obscured.

And wrecks passed without sound of bells,
The calyx of death's bounty giving back
A scattered chapter, livid hieroglyph,
The portent wound in corridors of shells.

Then in the circuit calm of one vast coil,
Its lashings charmed and malice reconciled,
Frosted eyes there were that lifted altars;
And silent answers crept across the stars.

Compass, quadrant and sextant contrive
No farther tides . . . High in the azure steeps
Monody shall not wake the mariner.
This fabulous shadow only the sea keeps.*

It is a difficult poem, certainly, but an interesting
one. I do not put it forward as one of his best, but
because of what he said about it. The editor who
first printed the poem was puzzled, and wrote to the
poet for enlightenment, as we would often like to do.
'Take me for a hard-boiled unimaginative unpoetic
reader,' he said, 'and tell me how *dice* can *bequeath an
embassy* (or anything else); and how a *calyx* (*of death's
bounty* or anything else) can give back a *scattered chapter,
livid hieroglyph*; and how, if it does, such a portent can
be *wound in corridors* (of shells or anything else). And
so on. I find your image of *frosted eyes lifting altars*
difficult to visualise. Nor do compass, quadrant and
sextant *contrive* tides, they merely record them, I
believe. Your ideas and rhythms interest me, and I
am wondering by what process of reasoning you would

* Copyright 1933 by Liveright, Inc.

justify this poem's succession of champion mixed metaphors of which you must be conscious.'

This sounds a little like the letter which Dr. Johnson did not write to Thomas Gray about his *Odes*, and many people must have felt like this during the past thirty-six years. What did the poet answer? Remember the subject, Herman Melville, the author of *Moby Dick*, remember the turmoil the reading of *Moby Dick* produces, even in an ordinary mind, remember how it led D. H. Lawrence into nightmare speculations, and then ask if it is inappropriate for the poet to take his imagery from the tortured mysteries of the sea.

The poet wrote in reply: 'I'll come to the explanations you requested on the Melville poem:

> Often beneath the wave, wide from this ledge
> The dice of drowned men's bones he saw bequeath
> An embassy.

Dice bequeath an embassy, in the first place, by being ground (in this connection only, of course) in little cubes from the bones of drowned men by the action of the sea, and are finally thrown up on the sand, having "numbers" but no identification. These being the bones of dead men who never completed their voyage, it seems legitimate to refer to them as the only surviving evidence of certain messages undelivered, mute evidence of certain things, experiences that the dead mariners might have had to deliver. Dice as a symbol of chance and circumstance is also implied.' Then, after other matters, he turns to the lines,

> Compass, quadrant and sextant contrive
> No farther tides'—

which had puzzled the editor, who had written, they don't '*contrive* tides, they merely record them'. The poet answered with indignation: 'Hasn't it often occurred that instruments originally invented for record and computation have inadvertently so extended the concepts of the entity they were invented to measure (concepts of space, etc.) in the mind and imagination that employed them, that they may metaphorically be said to have extended the original boundaries of the entity measured? This little bit of "relativity" ought not to be discredited in poetry now that scientists are proceeding to measure the universe on principles of pure *ratio*, quite as metaphorical, so far as previous standards of scientific methods extended.'

I wish this kind of comment were more frequent and more accessible in this country. We want more inside information, even if the poet sometimes proves that our guess is as good as his. It frequently should be as good, if the right kind of communication has been established. It can only be better than his when the poem has had time to reverberate in the civilisation of which it is one of the roots as well as one of the flowers. It is the poet who must tell us the direction in which he is going, and the more signposts on the road the more grateful we are.

One of the best of these signposts is a remarkable essay by Mr. Louis MacNeice on *Poetry To-day*, published in 1935 when the Auden, Spender, Day-Lewis group were beginning to dominate the scene. It is modest in tone, which is unusual in such things, and it discusses the *job* of poetry, which is also unusual, and it opens with a profound statement. 'Poets do not know (exactly) what they are doing, for if they did, there would be no need to do it.' But he soon clarifies and qualifies this by saying that 'People will not read poetry unless they think they know what they are going to get from it, and people will not write poetry unless they think they know what they are driving at'. Between these two statements lies the mystery of the process of poetry, whether in our own time or any other. The trouble with our own age is that it is a morbidly self-conscious age. We want to know what we are doing *while* we are doing it. We shout about the unconscious, but we do not trust it. We want to have it both ways. The poet *should* trust his unconscious, whether he afterwards conducts a court-martial on its activities or not.

The finest inquiry of this kind I know is a detailed analysis of the *Birth of a Poem* by the late Robert Nichols, printed as an appendix to Rosamond Harding's *An Anatomy of Inspiration*. It is the most detailed description in existence of the genesis and progress of a poem, a romantic poem, an old-fashioned poem if you like, or a perennially fashionable poem if you like, an apparently straightforward poem, and it may one day be as important as Edgar Allan Poe's account of the composition of *The Raven*, as well as being, I think, more honest and more informative.

He describes, among other things, how a slight alteration made a line take shape. 'No sooner had this change been effected,' he wrote, 'than I recognised that the line had *set* in an order that no subsequent occurrence must be suffered to disturb. When a line is once really right its rightness is of so sacrosanct a nature that rather than change it the poet . . . will abandon the entire piece.   The laws of psychological necessity within the art are absolutely inflexible and the poet's personal integrity is involved in his recognition of and reverence for the fact that a line is right and that nothing in heaven or earth can make it otherwise. If it is changed it may be right for some poem or other, but that poem will not be the poem originally intended.'

Sometimes we have a clue to the chasm between rightness and wrongness in a poetical line, the gulf between groping statement and what we sometimes call 'inevitability', when we see a poet's corrected manuscript.   The manuscripts of Milton's *Minor Poems* at Cambridge are chock-full of such instances, and the manuscript of Keats's *Ode to a Nightingale* tells us that

> Charm'd *magic* casements, opening on the foam
> Of *perilous* seas, in faery lands forlorn.

was once '*the wide* casements, opening on the foam Of *keelless* seas', and the '*song* that found a path Through the sad heart of Ruth' was originally 'the *voice* that found a path'.

Such inevitabilities are the result, not of directions and movements, but the work of individuals.   Literary historians are interested in movements, because such a schematisation makes their work easier.   Many years ago I tried to establish a distinction between two kinds of literature; the labels I applied were— 'the literature of *achievement*' and 'the literature of *direction*'.   Such a distinction is of some importance for the literary historian.   He must try to see what is permanent and valuable, and what is merely symptomatic. The symptoms are most clearly seen in minor literature, and that is why the literary historian so frequently delights in studying minor literature, because it is clearer and more instructive, *not* because he cannot tell the difference between major and minor writing.

Is there any individual achievement in our own time, apart from the eddy of directions? How can we recognise it? In other words, what is poetry? If I wanted to be flippant, without for one moment ceasing to be serious, I should say that poetry, whatever else it may or may not be, is something which defies the efforts of Mr. William Empson to resolve it into his seven or fifty-seven varieties of ambiguity. In short, everything I have been saying hitherto has been beside the point. Movements, symbolism, imagism, the relation of poetry and science, are only a background of 'direction'. For scrutiny of the foreground we need a touchstone of achievement, we need something to help us detect the accent of authenticity.

I am going to lay myself wide open. I want poetry like Burns's poem:

> O my luve's like a red, red rose,
>   That's newly sprung in June:
> O my luve's like the melodie
>   That's sweetly play'd in tune.

Or like William Blake's:

> Tiger! Tiger! burning bright
> In the forests of the night.

Or Wordsworth's inevitability:

> No motion has she now, no force;
>   She neither hears nor sees;
> Rolled round in earth's diurnal course,
>   With rocks, and stones, and trees.

These are not simple poems, they only seem to be
simple. 'Rolled round in earth's diurnal course' has
as close relation to changes of astronomical feeling as
any of John Donne's, but each of these poems is a
perfect mould of music into which the meaning fits
by being part of the music. I want musical poetry,
which is by no means the same thing as melodious
poetry.

Some of the clearest statements on this vexed question
of music have been made by Mr. T. S. Eliot in his not
widely enough known lecture on *The Music of Poetry*.
'The music of a word,' he says, 'arises from its relation
first to the words immediately preceding and following
it, and indefinitely to the rest of its context; and from
another relation, that of its immediate meaning in
that context to all the other meanings which it has had
in other contexts, to its greater or less wealth of association'; and he says that a 'musical poem' is one 'which
has a musical pattern of sound and a musical pattern
of the secondary meanings of the words which compose
it, and that these two patterns are indissoluble and
one'. And he makes a valuable confession, both
personally and on behalf of his craft, when he says, 'I
know that a poem, or a passage of a poem, may tend
to realise itself first as a particular rhythm before it
reaches expression in words, and that this rhythm may

bring to birth the idea and the image; and I do not believe that this is an experience peculiar to myself'. It is indeed not peculiar to Mr. Eliot. In one of Shelley's notebooks I have found an entry where the first draft of one of his finest poems consists only of a rhythmical scheme held in place by a sequence of completely meaningless syllables.

I like the work of some of my contemporaries not only because their poems move me, often for private and extraneous reasons, but because I feel through them a sense of the world in which we have grown up together, and a proof that we have not grown up in vain in this world; because they have included some-thing which has taken poetry further on its path, a continuation of the broadening path of tradition which the poets have followed unbrokenly; because they have as individual voices in our own time as Shakespeare had in his day.

> Being your slave what should I do but tend,
> Upon the hours, and times of your desire?
> I have no precious time at all to spend;
> Nor services to do till you require.
> Nor dare I chide the world-without-end hour,
> Whilst I (my sovereign) watch the clock for you.

Yet this, no more than Beethoven's melody, was not achieved without manœuvring for perfect position. We have Beethoven's notebooks, and we have Shake-speare's rough drafts to prove this. And because Shakespeare was a craftsman and grappled with his time, and was no God out of heaven, I think it fair to measure the new-comers by him.

Robert Frost is such an individual, an American, one of the greatest of living poets, aware of his age, yet speaking in his own voice he can give us the kind of inevitability I seek.

> The way a crow
> Shook down on me
> The dust of snow
> From a hemlock tree
>
> Has given my heart
> A change of mood
> And saved some part
> Of a day I had rued.*

This is Georgian poetry, at its very best, and I am glad to be able to offer wholeheartedly a specimen of a movement so often betrayed by its members. Robert Frost influenced English poetry through that fine writer Edward Thomas.

I have often thought that in the final essence, paradoxical as it may seem, all poetry is about poetry, that there is some meaning in the phrase 'poetry for poetry's sake', not in the æsthete's sense of the poet taking refuge in poetry from the encroaching dangers of life, but in the sense that the poet's prime justification for being in this world is his endeavour to master it, to struggle until he has subdued it, until he has reshaped its incoherences and tensions, other people's shapes and forces, perhaps even God (the rival creator)'s shapes, into his own coherences and harmonies. Whether he take his starting-point from the little Celandine, the tiger, the red rose, the myth of Prometheus or the Copernican universe, it is this coherence and harmony he is really writing about.

* Copyright 1923, by Henry Holt & Co., Inc., 1951 by Robert Frost

Sometimes he shows you the coherent result, sometimes he can only stammer, 'You see what I mean, it's like so-and-so and so-and-so.' The images fall apart, the centre cannot hold. I must finish sometime an anthology on which I have been working for years, of *Poems on Poetry*. Here, by one of the greatest of American poets, perhaps *the* greatest, Mr. Wallace Stevens, is a poem called *Of Modern Poetry*.* He is a poet who insists, by the disposition of the words on the printed page, on the way he wants the poem read.

> The poem of the mind in the act of finding
> What will suffice.   It has not always had
> To find: the scene was set; it repeated what
> Was in the script.
>   Then the theatre was changed
> To something else.   Its past was a souvenir.
>
> It has to be living, to learn the speech of the
>   place.
> It has to face the men of the time and to meet
> The women of the time.   It has to think about
>   war
> And it has to find what will suffice.   It has
> To construct a new stage. ᐧ   It has to be on that
>   stage
> And, like an insatiable actor,   slowly   and
> With meditation, speak words that in the ear,
> In the delicatest ear of the mind,   repeat,
> Exactly, that which it wants to hear, at the sound
> Of which, ᐧan invisible audience listens,
> Not to the play, but to itself, expressed
> In an emotion as of two people, as of two

* Reprinted from *Parts of a World* by Wallace Stevens by permission of the publisher, Alfred A. Knopf, Inc. Copyright 1942 by Wallace Stevens.

Emotions becoming one.´   The actor is
A metaphysician in the dark, twanging
An instrument, twanging a wiry string that gives
Sounds passing through sudden rightnesses, wholly
Containing the mind, below which it cannot
   descend,
Beyond which it has no will to rise.
                              It must
Be the finding of a satisfaction; and may
Be of a man skating, a woman dancing, a woman
Combing.   ´The poem of the act of the mind.´

By contrast there is an English confession of poetic
faith, by Alun Lewis, who was killed in the war.   It
is called *The Poet.* *

Five slender birches grouped in peace,
Five silver boles at the end of the wood, lifting a
   green head.
The thunder breaks across them in the pent-up
   sky.
And I, uncomfortably feeling the sky's need,
Cannot sense the slenderness of the five birches.

Then the liberation of rain on the parched leaves,
On the cracked thunder lips,
On the scorched breath of lightning,
—Ceasing—
and leaving to me the five birches.

Poetry need not be epic, not even fiercely lyrical, to be
individual, it needs not the sun and the moon and the
stars.   It can be made up of odds and ends, as in this
poem with that very title, *Odds and Ends*.

The odds and ends of Autumn-swollen flies
Squat on the heavy fruits my mirrors double:

* Copyright 1942, by The Macmillan Company

The scattered firewood leaning in the dust
Of empty coal-bins: piled white rubble
Of summer cards and letters: speckled rust
On grate and poker: curtain poles that creak
When fingers twitch the curtains: oyster-skies
Along whose misty edges the trees rise
Like girders twisted in a hurricane:
Leaves at ballet-practice: and the old train
Of worn-out images in the lumbered brain. . . .

    All day I tried to bully my dead mood
    To yield the sweet nostalgia that's my due
    (So says my memory choked with odds and
       ends
    Of what it thinks it felt). All day I knew
    That it was neap-tide at the far grey flats
    And winter-solstice in my solitude,
    And in that bleakness lay reality.
    Yet for the sake of what past memory lends
    Of pain in amber, there I could not free
    The urgent skeleton from the glutton-fats.
    I wanted yashmak-veils of fine white sleep:
    Low orange-suns, and lovely lavender-calls:
    The snug warm hugging sense of winter near:
    Coals in the grate combing their smooth
      bright hair:
    Porcelain-cold by the sills where the leaves
      heap
    And the night falls. . . .

See how they come, the changeling images leap
Out of the cavernous mind! How can I keep
To the courage of urgent things that necessity,
Knowing no roots except in the depths of sleep
When dreams are turned as ploughs turn soil to
    the sun,
Stencils upon my frame as sun-frond the sky?

How can I task despair and life to be one
And keep the edge and brightness of the sense
Like featureless water, old with innocence?

That poem, which I choose for its note of
individuality, is from *Christ in the Synagogue*, by Mr.
L. Aaronson, a poet read mainly by other poets.

I have tried to make my points indirectly, to suggest,
almost by elimination, the qualities which constitute
achievement, the qualities which make for individuality.
Others too have been forced to deal in negatives, and in
order to praise a modern poem, Mr. Frank Kendon,
whose work I respect, had to describe it as 'surprisingly
free from science, obscurity, Eliotism, or nightmare
introspection'. But let me be a little more positive.
I find this quality of individual achievement cuts
right across the schools. It is to be seen in the work
of the poets I have quoted, Frost, Stevens and Aaronson,
in Wilfred Owen and Isaac Rosenberg, in Robert
Graves and Edmund Blunden, in John Crowe Ransom
and Andrew Young, in Edith Sitwell and in many
others, not forgetting W. B. Yeats and T. S. Eliot,
W. H. Auden and Dylan Thomas.

I must let the last word be from Mr. T. S. Eliot.
I am sorry to be compelled to quote so often from his
critical work, but I do so for three very good reasons:
first, because he has said more true, and now obvious,
things about poetry than anybody since Coleridge;
second, because, even when the ideas are my own, I
cannot be sure of not finding them later in some essay
of his I have never read; and finally, because he
speaks, as I cannot, with the authority of a poet,
and in that capacity he has something personal to

say about the direction which this achievement must take:

'That at which I have long aimed, in writing poetry; to write poetry which should be essentially poetry, with nothing poetic about it, poetry standing naked in its bare bones, or poetry so transparent that we should not see the poetry, but that which we are meant to see through the poetry, poetry so transparent that in reading it we are intent on what the poem *points at*, and not on the poetry, this seems to me the thing to try for.'